WHAT ARE THEY SAYING ABOUT MATTHEW?

What Are They Saying About Matthew?

Donald Senior, C.P.

PAULIST PRESS
New York/Ramsey

Library of Congress
Catalog Card Number: 82-62967

ISBN: 0-8091-2541-2

Published by Paulist Press
545 Island Road, Ramsey, New Jersey 07446

Printed and bound in the
United States of America

Contents

Preface

To understand "what they are saying about Matthew" it is important to understand what has been said about the Gospels in general in the past thirty years. The post-World War II period which saw such revolutionary changes in our Western culture also witnessed radically new ways of understanding the role of the evangelists and the nature of the Gospels they produced.

These new perspectives, like the broader changes in post-war society, did not appear out of thin air; they had been brewing in biblical scholarship for decades.[1] In the early part of the twentieth century, so-called "form critics" had concentrated on the period between the life of Jesus and the writing of the Gospels. Their interest was on the impact of the early Christian community on the development of the Gospel materials. Biblical scholars categorized the various "forms" the Gospel material took because of its use and preservation in different activities or settings of the early Church such as preaching, liturgy, conflicts, etc. But this focus tended to push the work of the evangelists themselves into the shadows. They were considered as mere "collectors" or editors of the Gospel materials.

But a new generation of biblical scholars was not content with that conclusion. Pioneers such as Willie Marxsen in his study of Mark's Gospel (1956) and Hans Conzelmann on the Gospel of Luke (1953) and Gunther Bornkamm on Matthew (1948) recognized that the evangelists contributed much more to the present form of the Gospels than merely assembling already existing materials; the evangelists brought new meaning and even content to the Gospel tradition.[2] From this conviction the method of "redaction criticism" was

1

born ("redaction" being an anglicized version of the German word *Redaktion* or "editing").

Redaction criticism, then, focuses on the contributions of the evangelist. Even though the Gospel material had been preserved in the early Church, the contribution of the Gospel writers was considerable. Not only did the evangelist assemble the contents of the Gospel, but he gave this material new meaning by selecting it, putting it into an overall narrative framework, and shaping the material anew with his own perspective. Each of the four Gospels is distinct because each evangelist, working in the milieu of a specific Christian community, added a new layer of interpretation to the traditions about Jesus.

More recent developments in Gospel studies tend to amplify the fundamental insight of redaction criticism: the evangelists not only collect and hand on traditional materials but are true authors in their own right. In this line, some biblical scholars prefer to use the term "composition criticism" rather than "redaction criticism."[3] They suggest that before comparing and contrasting a Gospel with parallel passages in other Gospels, it should first be viewed as an independent whole, with its own structure and meaning. More and more, analysts of the Gospels appeal to the insights of literary criticism: if an evangelist can be considered a true author, then the dynamics and procedures that effect all literary activity should be present in the Gospels and their impact on the reader.[4] The emphasis on the Gospels as literature coincides with a whole new appreciation in theology and biblical studies for the power of metaphorical language and of narrative to convey religious experience.[5]

Redaction criticism has been the dominant method in Matthean studies in the past thirty years, and that dominance will be reflected in the authors and issues of our review of recent scholarship.

Each chapter that follows takes its cue from the procedures and interests of Matthean scholarship. The first chapter concentrates on the possible milieu of Matthew's community—an important issue if, as redaction criticism claims, the evangelist shaped his Gospel in response to the circumstances of his community. The second chapter reviews the question of what sources Matthew may have used in the composition of the Gospel and what structure he gave his overall narrative—again both question important leads for discovering Matthew's message.

Subsequent chapters focus on major aspects of Matthew's theology: his view of salvation history, his interpretation of the Old Testament, his attitude toward the Jewish law, his Christology, and his ecclesiology or theology of the Church. Here the reader should be aware that this list of issues is limited and, to some extent, subjective. Few scholars, I believe, would deny that these topics are major questions in Matthew's Gospel; the flood of articles and books under each of these headings is testimony to this. But, undoubtedly, more issues could be added to the list such as Matthew's eschatology, his view of mission, and so on. And even such an expanded list would not include the many studies that have appeared on specific passages or more confined issues within the Gospel.[6]

But within the limits of our book (and its author) the topics included seemed the most crucial, the most comprehensive, and the ones that can give the reader a sense of how contemporary scholarship views the Gospel. Where possible, I have tried to use authors whose works are available in English to represent a specific position so that the interested reader could follow up, if he or she chose to. And to the extent I could restrain myself, I let the authors speak for themselves, although my own evaluations and prejudices are, I'm sure, apparent in most cases.

Writing this brief volume has been a pleasant task. Going back over the fertile soil of Matthean studies reminded me how subtle and magnetic is the Gospel that inspired all that scholarship. It also renewed a sense of gratitude I felt toward my mentor, Professor Frans Neirynck of the University of Louvain, who led me into the world of critical exegesis some fifteen years ago.

I suspect that if a similar review of Matthean studies is written a decade or so from now new things will have been said about Matthew, especially from the insights of literary criticism. As I point out occasionally in the chapters ahead, redaction criticism itself pushes in that direction. But at this moment in the history of biblical scholarship, "what they are saying about Matthew" is, I hope, fairly represented in these pages.

1
The Setting for Matthew's Gospel

Introduction

Like skilled preachers, the evangelists told their stories of Jesus in such a way that they would touch the concerns and hopes of their audience. Therefore one of the major interests of redaction criticism has been to determine the milieu of the community for which a particular Gospel was written. This has certainly been the case with studies on the Gospel of Matthew.

It is important to remember that practically speaking the exclusive source for gathering information about the circumstances of Matthew's community is the *Gospel* itself. We have no outside information from this early period which tells us who wrote Matthew's Gospel or what the problems were in his community. We do have rabbinical texts that tell us something about the situation of Judaism in the first century, but these texts were edited later than the Gospels and must be used with caution when we are attempting to get a picture of this earlier period. Through the writings of Eusebius (A.D. 260–339) we also have the comments of Papias who lived in the early part of the second century, but we cannot be sure that Papias himself had solid historical information about the author of the Gospel.[1]

Our best source for determining the situation in which Matthew wrote his Gospel remains, therefore, the Gospel itself. A good portion of Matthean studies in the past twenty-five years has concentrated on this question.

5

Matthew and Pharisaic Judaism

One of the most influential studies of Matthew's milieu is found in the book of W. D. Davies, *The Setting of the Sermon on the Mount.*[2] As its title indicates, this book attempts to situate the Sermon on the Mount in the wider context not only of Matthew's Gospel but of Judaism and the early Church. One of Davies' major conclusions was that Matthew's Sermon on the Mount and much of the rest of the Gospel was formulated in direct confrontation with Pharisaic Judaism. This conclusion has become an important consensus point in contemporary Matthean studies.

Davies begins by reconstructing the situation of Judaism after the dramatic events of the Jewish revolt against Rome and the resulting destruction of Jerusalem and the temple in A.D. 70. Historical sources for this period are murky but the general lines of the story can be pieced together. The strongest leadership group to survive this holocaust were the Pharisees, a lay reform movement that had been only one among many groups in Judaism prior to the revolt.[3] Under the leadership of Rabbi Johannan ben Zakkai the Pharisees would be the ones to draw Jewish life out of the ashes.

Johannan was not in sympathy with the Zealot group that had led the armed revolt against Rome nor with the Essenes who had counseled complete withdrawal from the social and political scene. His more pragmatic middle course opened a way to survival. He gathered a group of scholars at Jamnia near the Mediterranean coast. Here the foundations for rabbinic Judaism would be laid. The "academy" of Jamnia offset fragmentation within Judaism by asserting the rabbis' authority as interpreters of the law and regulators of Jewish life. The village synagogue was the Pharisees' base of power. Strict observance of the law replaced the central role that the liturgical life of the temple had played in Judaism. The Jewish law would eventually be codified and the canon of Jewish Scriptures formalized.

Jamnia also established a bulwark against external threats to Jewish life. Strict norms for Jewish identity were asserted to ward off the influence of pagans or of groups considered heretical. It is here, according to Davies, that Christianity came into the picture. Prior to the revolt Jewish Christians had remained within the broad boundaries of Judaism. But in the atmosphere of consolidation inaugurated by Jamnia this was no longer tolerable. The Jewish Christians, along with other groups considered heretical by the rabbis, were expelled from the synagogue. An important device for this was the insertion of the famous twelfth benediction into the *Tiffilah* or synagogue prayers, a reform instituted about A.D. 85. An ancient version of that prayer was discovered several years ago in the Cairo Genizah: "For persecutors let there be no hope, and the dominion of arrogance do Thou speedily root out in our days; and let Christians and *minim* (probably meaning 'heretics') perish in a moment, let them be blotted out of the book of the living and let them not be written with the righteous."[4] If anyone hesitated to read that prayer or to say "Amen" to it, they were liable to expulsion from the synagogue. The result was obvious. Although prior to the events of A.D. 70 the Jewish Christians had been part of Jewish liturgical and synagogue life, that was no longer possible in the atmosphere of strict identity set up by Jamnia. As Davies points out, it was not a matter of arbitrary hostility on the part of the rabbis, but a question of concern for their own identity and survival.

Davies is convinced that Matthew's Gospel, especially the Sermon on the Mount, was "a Christian response to Jamnia" (p. 315). Matthew's church, a majority of whose members were Jewish Christians, was concerned about its own identity now that it was cut off from its Jewish roots and being absorbed into the Gentile world. Matthew, therefore, attempted to define Christian identity over against the reform of Jamnia.

In Davies' opinion evidence of this "great gulf . . . between the Christian community and the synagogue" (p. 286) is found throughout the Gospel. Matthew refers to Jewish attacks on the report of Jesus' resurrection in 28:15. He often labels the synagogues as *"their synagogues"* (4:23; 9:35; 10:17; 12:9; 13:54). The "Pharisees" seem to be singled out as the group most hostile to the Matthean Jesus (5:20; 16:11–12; and especially 23:1–36).

Matthew also takes up many of the issues that were of concern to the rabbis at Jamnia. He alludes to the fall of Jerusalem (22:7) and to the infidelity of that city (23:37; 16:21; 21:10; 28:11; 27:58). In the infancy narrative and in the resurrection account he seems to favor

Galilee as the place of redemption instead of Jerusalem the unfaithful city, a stance that would be in opposition to that of the rabbis who were suspicious of radical movements in Galilee. The Matthean Jesus is openly critical of the ways of piety dear to the rabbis (see 6:25–34). Matthew's version of the Lord's Prayer may even be in conscious opposition to the elaborate synagogue prayer, the *Shemonah Esreh*. And, above all, Matthew's formulation of the antitheses ("You have heard it said, but *I* say to you"—see 5:22–48) in the Sermon on the Mount pits the "Torah" of Jesus against the Pharisees' interpretation of the law.

In Davies' view these and other special emphases of Matthew's Gospel indicate that the evangelist formulated his Gospel in a conscious dialectic with Jamnia. Matthew's community was probably located in Syria, an area which included a significant Jewish population and which was of special concern to the rabbis at Jamnia. Matthew was attempting to assist his own Christians to survive the wrenching pain of transition by clearly affirming the authority and authenticity of Jesus' own teaching and at the same time countering the attacks from the synagogue.

Although some scholars have disagreed with Davies' interpretation of Matthew and have questioned the extent and influence of the Jamnia reform, the majority has concurred with his basic position about the setting of Matthew's Gospel. Matthew wrote his Gospel during the critical transition period after the fall of Jerusalem and parallel to the formation of rabbinic Judaism.

Matthew's Church: In or Out of the Synagogue?

Some scholars have attempted to further specify the relationship between Matthew's church and the synagogue. Was the Gospel written after the break with the synagogue had become definitive—that is, sometime after the expulsion formalized in the mid-80's of the first century? Or was it written during a period of growing tension when the Jewish Christians were still involved in synagogue life but moving gradually toward separation, that is, sometime between A.D. 70 and 85?

In a study composed at the same time as that of W. D. Davies, a

German scholar, Reinhart Hummel, championed the second view: namely that Matthew's church had not yet definitively broken with the synagogue.[5] He readily admits that Matthew's Jewish Christians were in conflict with the Pharisees but at the time of the writing of the Gospel that conflict was still an intra-family debate. In fact, Hummel thought that Matthew was also in conflict with some Christians who were opposed to the law altogether.[6] Thus the evangelist was fighting a war on two fronts.

Hummel finds support for his view in the Gospel itself. The story about paying the temple tax in 17:24–27 is one bit of evidence. Hummel believes that Matthew writes after the destruction of the temple in A.D. 70. Even though the temple tax story stems from an earlier tradition, it still indicates that Matthew's community did not want to "scandalize" (17:27) Pharisaic Judaism. The exhortation in 23:2–3 to "practice and observe" whatever the scribes and Pharisees teach because they "sit on Moses' seat" is another indication that no definitive break with Judaism had yet occurred. Unlike Luke (6:32) and John (9:22; 12:42; 16:2) Matthew has no explicit references to exclusion from the synagogue. Warnings about persecution *in* the synagogues, on the other hand, imply that Matthew's church members still belonged (10:17; 23:34).

While Matthew's community is still part of the synagogue, this is an uneasy relationship. The evangelist is critical of the spirit of the Pharisees and contrasts it with Jesus' interpretation of the law which puts mercy as supreme (9:13; 12:7; 22:40). But some of the conflicts over law in the Gospel reflect *inner* community concerns. Matthew's church is a mixed church, composed of Jews and some Gentiles, a community in contact with Greek culture. From this milieu come "Hellenistic libertines" who dismiss the law altogether. But, in Hummel's view, Matthew's church developed its own style of piety which emphasized fidelity to the law. Thus Matthew warns his church against *anomia* or "lawlessness" (see 5:17–20; 7:12–17; 11:12–13; 24:10–13). Fidelity to Jesus as Messiah meant avoiding not only Pharisaic legalism but also any frivolous abandonment of the requirements of the law.

For Hummel, therefore, Matthew's community still belonged to the synagogue although the relationship was a turbulent one. At the same time, under the impact of the Jesus tradition and the influx of Gentile members, Matthew's church was developing its own style, distinct from that of Pharisaic Judaism. This independence would ultimately lead to a definitive break.

A majority of recent interpreters disagree with Hummel's analysis and are convinced that Matthew's community had already experienced a definitive rupture with Judaism. Evidence of respect for Pharisaic institutions singled out by Hummel are, in fact, vestiges of earlier stages in the development of Matthew's tradition. A representative of this viewpoint is Douglas Hare in his book *The Theme of Jewish Persecution of Christians in the Gospel According to St. Matthew.*[7] As the title of his study indicates, Hare's primary goal is to investigate the scope and nature of the persecution experienced by Christian missionaries, particularly in the post-70 period. Bitter texts such as Matthew 23:29–39 and 10:16–37 stem from the rejection of Christian missionaries by the synagogues of Pharisaic Judaism. This failure of the Christian mission to Israel had a deep influence on Matthew's sense of salvation history: now the offer of salvation was turned toward the Gentiles (28:16–20). Thus Matthew's community had experienced a painful and definitive rupture with Judaism.

In his important study of Matthew's theology entitled *Der Weg der Gerechtigkeit* ("The Way of Righteousness"), Georg Strecker asserted the same view: Matthew's community had made a definitive break with Judaism.[8] Strecker assembles an imposing list of evidence: Matthew speaks of *"their"* scribes (7:29) and *"their"* synagogues (4:23; 9:35; 10:17; 12:9; 13:54). In comparison to parallel passages in Mark and Luke, Matthew intensifies polemical references to the Pharisees (see 15:12–14; 23:25–26). The title *rabbi,* which is often used in Mark to refer respectfully to Jesus (Mk. 9:5; 11:21; 14:45), is found in Matthew only on the lips of Judas (26:25, 49). And the disciples are warned not to take on the title "rabbi" (23:7–8). These are clear signals of alienation from Pharisaic Judaism. At the same time Matthew shows an openness to the Gentiles (28:19; 21:43, etc.), a sharp contrast with his hostility to the leaders of Judaism.

Therefore, for Strecker, Hare, and a majority of Matthean interpreters the community that produced the Gospel had already severed its ties with Pharisaic Judaism, a wrenching break that left the imprint of its wounds on Matthew's theological perspective.

Jew or Gentile?

Given the fact that Matthew's Gospel seems to struggle with so many explicitly Jewish issues, most commentators assume that the evangelist himself was a Jewish Christian. Hummel, for example, considers Matthew to be a converted scribe of the Pharisee party.[9] Hare suggests that the bitter tones in Matthew's references to Judaism are due to the pain of separation from his own people.[10]

But some recent studies maintain that even though Matthew's community had Jewish-Christian roots, the evangelist himself was a Gentile. An early defender of this position was the Swedish author Poul Nepper-Christensen in his book, *Das Matthäusevangelium. Ein judenchristliches Evangelium?*[11] A more recent proponent is John Meier in his study of Matthew's theology entitled *The Vision of Matthew: Christ, Church and Morality in the First Gospel.*[12] He notes that Matthew's antagonism to Pharisaic Judaism is hard to reconcile with Jewish authorship. Meier points to such texts as the denunciation of the Jewish leaders in chapters 15 and 23 and 27:25 where the "whole people" accept responsibility for the innocent blood of Jesus. Meier also contends that on occasion Matthew makes errors about things Jewish. For example, the evangelist seems to be confused about the differences between the Sadducees and the Pharisees. In 16:6 and 12, for example, Matthew refers to the "leaven of the Pharisees and Sadducees" (in contrast to Mark 8:15 which states the "leaven of the Pharisees and the leaven of *Herod*"). The evangelist explicitly interprets "leaven" as a metaphor for their "teaching" (Mt. 16:12). The problem is that these two groups did not share a uniform "teaching" or "doctrine," as Matthew's phrase implies. On such key issues as the interpretation of law and the doctrine of resurrection the Sadducees and Pharisees were at loggerheads. Meier believes further ambiguity about the Sadducees can be detected in Matthew 22:23 where instead of the historically precise identification of the Sadducees as those "who say there is no resurrection" (as in Mark 12:18 and Luke 20:27) Matthew's text reads, ". . . Sadducees, *saying* there is no resurrection," as if this were the conviction of some particular Sadducees and not the tenet of the entire party.

Meier sees another Matthean "error" in his excessively literal reading of Zechariah 9:9 in the account of Jesus' triumphant entry into Jerusalem. In Matthew's rendition of the scene (again in contrast to the parallel in Mark 11:1–10), the disciples are instructed to prepare "an ass . . . and a colt" and Jesus sits on *both* (cf. Mt. 21:7)! Commentators have traditionally explained this as Matthew's attempt to see a literal fulfillment of Zechariah 9:9 in this event of Jesus' life. Meier, however, thinks this also shows that Matthew misunderstands the Hebrew parallelism of Zechariah 9:9 where the reference to a donkey and a colt is not to two animals, but to *one*. Meier contends that only someone unfamiliar with Hebrew poetic forms, and, therefore, not a Jew, would be this literal on such an insignificant detail. Therefore, Matthew was not a Jew who became a Christian but a Gentile Christian who became well versed in the Hebrew Scriptures and things Jewish.

The debate on this issue is not closed, but it should be noted that a majority of scholars continue to maintain that the evangelist was a Jewish Christian. The Gospel's occasional bitter critique of the Jewish leaders can be explained by the rupture between the Church and the synagogue. And Matthew's alleged "errors" are extremely subtle. As we shall note below, many scholars locate Matthew's church in Hellenistic or disapora Judaism, somewhere in the Roman empire outside of Palestine. Therefore Matthew was somewhat removed from the culture and circumstances of the Judaism Jesus knew.

Where? When? and Who?

Scholarship continues its sleuth work on these traditional questions about the origin of the Gospel. Classical assumptions about Matthew were that it was the first Gospel written, was authored by the apostle Matthew, and was, therefore, written somewhere in Palestine. All of these assumptions have been challenged.

The conclusions of Jack Dean Kingsbury in his introductory volume on the Gospel offer a good synthesis of representative critical scholarship.[13] Kingsbury suggests that Matthew's community may have been located in Antioch of Syria, where there was a mixed population of Jews and Gentiles. The probable date of the Gospel is

around A.D. 85 or 90, some twenty years after the destruction of Jerusalem (A.D. 70), which Matthew alludes to in 22:7, and after the
writing of Mark's Gospel which Matthew seems to have used as a
source.[14]

Kingsbury bases these conclusions on the profile that begins to
emerge from a close examination of the Gospel. First of all the language spoken by Matthew's community was Greek. The Greek style
of Matthew is of good quality, not the kind of "translation Greek"
that a native Hebrew or Aramaic speaker would be likely to use. At
the same time, the Jewish tone of Matthew's Gospel suggests that a
majority of his community was Greek-speaking Jews.

Kingsbury also believes that Matthew's church was "urban and
prosperous." Matthew refers to cities some twenty-six times and to
villages only four times (by contrast, Mark refers to cities eight times
and to villages seven times). Instead of simply the "poor" (Lk. 6:20)
Matthew's Jesus blesses the "poor *in spirit*" (5:3). And Matthew frequently escalates the value and amounts of money referred to in the
Gospel. For example in Mark 6:8 Jesus commands the disciples to
take "no copper coins" with them on their journeys; in Matthew's
version (10:9) that is inflated to no "gold, nor silver, nor copper
coin." Luke's parable of the *minas* (19:11–27) escalates in Matthew
to the parable of the *talents* (25:14–30), an amount fifty times more
valuable than a *minas*. In Mark (15:43) and Luke (23:50–51), Joseph
of Arimathea is identified as a member of the Sanhedrin, but Matthew describes Joseph as "a rich man . . . who was also a disciple of
Jesus" (27:57). In fact throughout his Gospel Matthew refers to
"gold" and "silver" more times than Mark and Luke combined.

Kingsbury allies himself with the opinion discussed above
which places Matthew's community outside of the synagogue.[15] Matthew's Jewish Christians had made a break with their counterparts in
Pharisaic Judaism and now a sizable number of Gentiles were members of the community as well. As Kingsbury puts it: "[The Matthean community is] a church with members of Jewish and Gentile
background which stands outside the orbit of official Judaism but
lives in close proximity to both Jews and Gentiles, [and] encounters
from without persecution on the part of both Jew and Gentile" (p.
101).

Antioch of Syria, a large urban center with a mixed population, seems to fit this description. But not all scholars agree that Antioch is the only possible place. A few have suggested Alexandria, mainly because of Matthew's tradition about the flight into Egypt in 2:13–15, or Phoenicia.[16] More recently the American scholar Benedict Viviano has put forward Caesarea Maritima, a lavish port city developed by Herod the Great, as a place which fulfills all the conditions reflected in the Gospel (urban, prosperous, mixed population).[17] In addition, Caesarea has the advantage of being in Palestine, thus locating Matthew's community closer to the center of the Pharisaic reform. Viviano also argues that Caesarea became one of the earliest and most vigorous centers of Christian learning, a possible explanation for the literary and theological sophistication of Matthew.[18]

Although the location of Matthew's church will continue to be debated, a stronger consensus about authorship has emerged to the extent that few scholars are willing to identify the evangelist with the apostle Matthew. Kingsbury's viewpoint is representative: The evangelist was most probably *not* the apostle because: (1) Matthew depends on Mark as his main source and, therefore, does not seem to be an eyewitness, (2) the theological concerns and perspectives of Matthew are those of a "second generation" Christian, and (3) if the Gospel is written around A.D. 85–90, the apostle Matthew was probably already dead.

However, the ancient Church tradition that assigned the Gospel to the apostle Matthew is not dismissed out of hand by Kingsbury and other recent scholars. The second century Church writer Papias asserted that "Matthew wrote the oracles in the Hebrew language and everyone interpreted them as he was able." As we will discuss below, this led to a hypothesis about an original Aramaic edition of the Gospel.[19] But Papias' information may not be accurate. In the Gospel itself is the intriguing text where Mark's account of the call of Levi (2:14) is changed in Matthew to the call of the tax collector *Matthew* (cf. 9:9). Matthew makes a corresponding change in his list of apostles in 10:3. Other evidence may rule out Matthew as the final author of the Gospel, but perhaps the apostle was associated in some way with the origin of Matthew's community. About this there can only be speculation.

Conclusion

Almost all of these hypotheses about the setting of Matthew's community point to a church in transition. The evangelist wrote for a group of Christians who were undergoing a transformation from a predominately Jewish–Christian church to an increasingly Gentile church, from a church whose roots and cultural origin were Palestinian to a church plunged into the midst of the Roman empire. The destruction of Jerusalem by the Romans signaled the end of the form of Judaism known to Jesus and to the earliest apostolic Church. Both Judaism and Jewish Christianity had to strike a new course. This search for identity and for continuity within discontinuity seems to have been one of the primary purposes of Matthew's Gospel.[20]

2
The Sources and Structure
of the Gospel

Introduction

This chapter considers two issues which probe beneath the surface of Matthew's Gospel: (1) On what sources did Matthew draw for the contents of his Gospel? (2) What plan or structure did he use to give shape to his story?

Both of these questions have been the focus of recent scholarship because attempting to answer those questions helps the reader of the Gospel determine the specific theological perspective of Matthew's text. We shall sample some of the scholarly work done in each area.

I. The Sources for Matthew's Gospel

At least from the time of Augustine of Hippo (fifth century) it was assumed that the canonical order of the Gospels—Matthew, Mark, Luke, John—was in fact their historical order. Matthew was considered to be the first Gospel written, its author an apostle and eyewitness to events of the Gospel.

But modern biblical scholarship has challenged these assumptions. In the latter part of the nineteenth century, scholars developed a hypothesis about the interrelationship of the Gospels which came to be known as the "two-source" theory.[1] Noting the striking similarities between Mark on the one hand and Matthew and Luke on the other, and the fact that Matthew and Luke had material in common but not present in Mark, scholars became convinced that Mark, not Matthew, was the first to be written. Matthew and Luke, independently of each other, used Mark as a primary source for their own versions of the Gospel. Matthew, for example, takes over more than 600 of Mark's 661 verses. In addition, Matthew and Luke (again independently of each other) had access to another "source" which was dubbed "Q" (after the German word *Quelle* or "source"). This material shared by Matthew and Luke was primarily sayings material (as, for example, much of the material in Matthew's Sermon on the Mount [ch. 5–7] and Luke's Sermon on the Plain [Lk. 6:17–49]) although it also contained parables (see the parable of the lost sheep in Mt. 18:12–13 and Lk. 15:3–7) and healing stories (compare Mt. 8:5–13 and Lk. 7:1–10). Authors speculated that the so-called "Q" document may have been a collection of Jesus' sayings that circulated among some of the early Christian communities. Opinion is divided on whether this collection was written or passed on orally.[2] At any rate, Q provided Matthew and Luke with important additional material for the revision of Mark's Gospel.

This, in very schematic form, is what is meant by the "two-source" theory: in composing this Gospel Matthew had access to two major sources, the Gospel of Mark and Q. Not all of the material in Matthew's narrative is accounted for by these two sources. There are a significant number of passages unique to Matthew such as the infancy narratives of chapters 1–2, the parable of the sheep and the goats in 25:31–46, or the account of the guards at the tomb in 27:62–66 and 28:11–15, and many more examples. Scholars debate whether these special stories come from some special source (sometimes designated as "M" for Matthew) or whether in some instances the evangelist drew the stories from the traditions of his church or even freely composed them himself.

The great majority of Matthean interpreters today accept the two-source theory as a working hypothesis, even though many of them admit that it does not explain all of the complex data of the Gospels' origin. By contrasting Matthew's rendition of a passage with his presumed source Mark or Q, the interpreter can detect what specific perspective the evangelist has introduced by means of his alterations, expansions or abbreviations. Thus the two-source theory has been the launching pad for many of the conclusions of redaction criticism.

For example, in a recent study defending the two-source theory, Gunther Bornkamm uses the so-called community discourse of chapter 18 as a test case.[3] He contends that the discourse is a "mosaic" of Matthew's sources: from Mark (compare Mt. 18:1–5 and Mk. 9:33–37; Mt. 18:6–9 and Mk. 9:42–48), from Q (the parable in Mt. 18:12–13, compare Lk. 15:3–7, and the sayings in 18:21–22, compare Lk. 17:4), and from Matthew's own special traditions (Mt. 18:15–17 and the concluding section on forgiveness, 18:23–35). Bornkamm is convinced that awareness of how Matthew combines and adapts the various sources brings the interpreter closer to Matthew's meaning in the passage. In my own work on Matthew's passion narrative I found the same striking confirmation of Matthew's dependence on Mark in a section of the Gospel where the two accounts are extremely similar.[4]

Challenges to the Two-Source Hypothesis

But in this issue, like most others, biblical scholarship does not walk in lockstep. There have been a number of recent challenges to the two-source theory.

Abbot B. C. Butler in his 1951 work *The Originality of St. Matthew*[5] attacked the two-source theory head-on. He maintained that Matthew's Gospel was the first and that it was the major source for Mark. Some Catholic authors such as Vosté had attempted to maintain the tradition of Matthew's priority by asserting that the original version (now lost) had been in Aramaic, not Greek. Mark's Greek version depended on this Aramaic Matthew, while the Greek edition of Matthew used both Aramaic Matthew and Mark. This hypothesis wanted to reconcile both camps—Matthean priority and a semblance of the two-source theory (with its Markan priority).

But Abbot Butler was much bolder. His hypothesis was that Mark depended directly on the *Greek* Gospel of Matthew. He also affirmed the tradition of Papias that connected the Gospel of Mark with Peter. The apostle used Matthew's text as his *aide-memoire,* selecting passages "which his own memory could confirm and enlarge upon," and omitting incidents "that occurred before he met our

Lord" (p. 168). In this way Butler hoped to circumvent a major objection to the theory of Matthean priority, that is, why Mark would eliminate from his narrative such major chunks of the Gospel of Matthew as the infancy narrative and the Sermon on the Mount.

Butler's hypothesis did not receive universal or enthusiastic acceptance, but it was not the last dissent to the two-source theory. An American scholar William R. Farmer mounted a systematic challenge to the prevailing consensus in his revival of the Griesbach hypothesis which claimed that Matthew wrote first and that Luke expanded on Matthew,[6] while Mark, in turn, used both Matthew and Luke in writing his Gospel.

A challenge in another direction came from Michael D. Goulder in his work *Midrash and Lection in Matthew.*[7] He affirms Matthew's literary dependence on Mark but denies that there was any Q source at all. Matthew, in Goulder's viewpoint, was extraordinarily creative; he did not depend on any special source other than Mark but freely composed those passages not found in Mark in order to serve the liturgical and catechetical needs of his church. Matthew, Goulder suggests, operated as a Christian scribe, expounding his interpretation of the Gospel as the Jewish scribes did of the Torah.

The challenges come full circle with a theory such as that proposed in the Anchor Bible commentary of W. F. Albright and C. S. Mann.[8] They question whether there is any direct literary relationship among the Synoptic Gospels at all and hold that a more probable explanation for the similarities among the three is the existence of a very early Aramaic or Hebrew Gospel which was the common source for all three of the evangelists.

Despite these and many other proposed solutions to the Synoptic problem, it remains true that the two-source theory is the dominant hypothesis among interpreters of Matthew's Gospel. The challenges, while failing to dissuade most exegetes from the two-source theory, do have some healthy effects. For one, they caution exegetes against making the two-source hypothesis an unchallengeable dogma. It is only a hypothesis and it does not explain everything about Matthew's use of sources with equal clarity (cf., for example, the question of the "minor agreements"—those cases where Matthew and Luke have identical wording in passages over against both Mark and Q).[9]

Secondly, the hypothetical nature of all theories about Matthew's use of sources has cautioned exegetes against relying too exclusively on such theories for an interpretation of Matthew's text. The ultimate goal of redaction criticism is not to catalogue Matthew's alterations of his source material but to appreciate the overall meaning of the text as we now have it. This point is made by William Thompson in his book *Matthew's Advice to a Divided Community: Mt. 17, 22–18, 35.*[10] There are two dimensions to the redaction critic's work: (1) "horizontal," in which the text of Matthew is compared with the parallel accounts of Mark and Luke in order to determine how Matthew has adapted his source material; (2) "vertical," that is, analyzing the style, structure and flow of an individual passage within the ongoing context of Matthew's Gospel. This vertical dimension is the more essential one, Thompson claims, because ". . . the evangelist's interpretation of tradition will ultimately emerge only from a study of individual pericopes in their own composition and in relation to their surrounding context and the gospel as a whole" (p. 9).

This attention to the literary features of the Gospel text allies redaction criticism with literary criticism, a growing force in modern biblical studies. The evangelists are not mere collectors of tradition but genuine authors, shaping their narratives from their own theological perspective and with their individual literary skill. The biblical scholar, therefore, should be sensitive to the literary dynamics of the biblical text.

II. The Structure of Matthew's Gospel

If Matthew is a genuine author, then we should expect his Gospel story to have all the elements of a story, including that of a "plot" or structure. What passages or features of Matthew's narrative tip us off to the way the evangelist intended to move his reader through the story? Wrestling with this question, too, can help us discover Matthew's intended meaning with more depth and precision. As in the question of sources no single solution has been found, but many of the proposed structures throw light on different facets of the Gospel. We will sample three attempts.

A. The Discourse Format

One of the most influential answers to the question of Matthew's structure was provided by an American scholar, Benjamin Bacon.[11] His so-called Pentateuchal theory is not widely accepted today, but Bacon highlighted certain aspects of Matthew's narrative that are featured in almost every attempt to solve the riddle of its structure.

Bacon noted the presence of a more or less fixed statement that occurred five times in Matthew's Gospel (7:28; 11:1; 13:53; 19:1; 26:1). Each of these statements begins in similar fashion (for example, "And when Jesus finished these sayings . . ."—Mt. 7:28) and each marks the boundary between a discourse section and a narrative section of the Gospel. This phenomenon led Bacon to propose that the structure of Matthew's Gospel was modeled after that of the five great books of the Pentateuch. Each of Matthew's "books" included both narrative and discourse (a pattern which Bacon felt could be traced in the five books of the Pentateuch as well), with the fivefold formula signaling the end of the discourse and, therefore, the end of each "book."

Matthew's intention, according to Bacon, was to present Jesus as a "new Moses," offering a new law to the Church. In this way, Bacon surmised, Matthew, a converted rabbi, hoped to counteract lawlessness in his own church.

Bacon's thesis was clear and attractive, but under close scrutiny it did not hold up. The important objection was that Bacon's five-book framework left out some crucial Matthean passages. Bacon had relegated the infancy narratives of chapters 1 and 2 and the passion and resurrection accounts of chapters 26–28 to "prologue" and "epilogue" respectively, because they did not fit into his five-book format. But these major parts of the Gospel hardly stand on the periphery of Matthew's story about Jesus! Bacon's proposal also overlooks other discourses present in Matthew which are not marked off by the five formulae, such as the speeches in 11:7–30 and 23:1–39. Secondly, it is not clear that the formula which Bacon believed concluded the books of Matthew is really a *concluding* formula at all. On face value those five verses seem more like transitional statements that move the reader along to the next section after a discourse is finished. And, finally, Bacon's theory suggested that Matthew wanted to depict Jesus as the "new Moses." But there is no real evidence that this was a major concern of Matthew.[12]

While Bacon's "Pentateuchal" structure is not accepted today, other scholars have tried variations on this theme. Hubert Frankemoëlle in a major study of Matthew's theology entitled *Jahwebund und Kirche Christi* ("Covenant of Yahweh and Church of Christ")[13] finds Old Testament inspiration for Matthew's discourses not in the fivefold structure of the Pentateuch but in the Book of Deuteronomy. Frankemoëlle notes the similarities between the transition formula, especially that of 26:1, and Deuteronomy 31:1, 24 and 32:44–45. Like Matthew's Gospel, Deuteronomy is a narrative interspersed with speeches; in fact the final formula is meant to bind together speech and narrative sections. And Moses' discourses, like that of Jesus in Matthew, end with warnings of judgment. Both Deuteronomy and Matthew emphasize the need to do good deeds. Frankemoëlle also sees a parallel in that Deuteronomy presents Moses as giving a series of farewell discourses to Israel as it stands on the brink of a new future; Matthew's Jesus seems to do the same thing for the Church. Thus Frankemoëlle uses the discourses to retrieve the Mosaic motif of Bacon's theory but, ultimately, on completely different grounds.

B. Chiastic Patterns

Everyone recognizes that Matthew brings more "order" to the Gospel material than the other evangelists. His grouping of Jesus' sayings into discourses, the collection of miracles in chapters 8 and 9, and judgment motifs in chapters 23–25 are evidence of this. Some scholars see Matthew's penchant for organization as a highly developed art leading to an intricate symmetrical pattern for the Gospel as a whole.

Peter F. Ellis, in his popular study *Matthew: His Mind and His Message,* has dubbed the evangelist "meticulous Matthew" and believes that the evangelist shaped his Gospel according to an intricate and comprehensive "chiastic" pattern.[14] Ellis agrees with Bacon and others that the sequence of narrative and discourse is important in Matthew's framework but the evangelist's overall plan is much more elaborate than Bacon had supposed.

First of all Ellis finds a symmetry running throughout the Gospel. Like a literary mobile Matthew's discourses "hang" from a center point, the parable discourse of chapter 13. In this suspension, discourses in the two halves of the Gospel parallel each other: the Sermon on the Mount of chapters 5–7 paralleling the judgment discourse of chapters 23–25; the mission discourse (chapter 10), in which the disciples are sent out, balanced by the community discourse (chapter 18), in which the "little ones" are received.

Ellis finds similar parallels in the narrative sections. For example the opening scenes of the Gospel (chapters 1–4) correspond with the passion and resurrection story (chapters 26–27) and so on. The "chiastic" form can be seen in the following diagram:

Sermon		(f) ch13 (f')
Narratives	ch 11–12 (e)	(e') ch 14–17
Sermons	ch 10 (d)	(d') ch 18
Narratives	ch 8–9 (c)	(c') ch 19–22
Sermons	ch 5–7 (b)	(b') ch 23–25
Narratives	ch 1–4 (a)	(a') ch 26–28[15]

Even this pattern does not exhaust Matthew's intricate planning in Ellis' view. He finds that the length of the discourses fits a pattern, too: the Sermon on the Mount roughly the same length as the discourse of chapters 23–25, and chapter 10 about the same length as chapter 18 and so on. Even the content of the discourses have thematic relationship, Ellis claims. For example, chapter 10 on the mission of the apostles parallels chapter 18's attention to the authority of the apostles within the community. In the first half of the Gospel (up to the mid-point of chapter 13) Jesus speaks to all the Jews; after 13:35 Jesus turns his attention to the disciples. And, finally, Matthew's use of numbers is significant. Ellis' proposed framework counts five great discourses and two minor ones (3:8–12; 28:18–20), adding up to seven, a highly symbolic number favored by Matthew.

Ellis' proposed structure has to be commended for its ingenuity but a close look at this framework raises some questions. For example, Ellis considers chapters 11–12 as a "narrative," when in fact it has a lot of discourse material (cf. 11:7–30), much more in fact, than what Ellis calls the "minor discourse" of 3:8–12 which is a discourse of John the Baptist, not Jesus. Several of the thematic relationships between sets of narratives or discourses seem quite tenuous, as that between the miracle chapters of 8–9 and the variety of materials in chapters 19–22, or between the mission discourse of chapter 10 and the community discourse of chapter 18. The parallels Ellis suggest are so subtle that one wonders if the evangelist intended to build his Gospel story in such a way.

C. "From that time . . ."

Other scholars find the key to Matthew's structure not in the narrative and discourse sequence but in another set of signals. Twice in his Gospel Matthew uses the phrase "From that time Jesus began . . ." (cf. 4:17 and 16:7). Some authors, such as Jack Dean Kingsbury, believe that this phrase marks the boundaries of the major divisions of the Gospel.[16] The words "from that time" show that by means of this formula the evangelist wanted to indicate "the beginning of a new phase in the life of Jesus" (p. 8). Each of the formula signals the major theme of the section it introduces. The formula in 4:17 reads, "From that time Jesus began to preach, saying, 'Repent, for the kingdom of heaven is at hand,' " thereby introducing that major section of the Gospel where Jesus' public proclamation is described. In 16:21 the formula reads, "From that time Jesus began to show his disciples that he must go to Jerusalem and suffer many things from the elders and chief priests and scribes, and be killed, and on the third day be raised," thus introducing the major part of the Gospel dealing with the suffering, death and resurrection of Jesus the Messiah.

To complete his outline Kingsbury has to contend with the section from chapter 1 up to 4:16. He believes that the opening verse of the Gospel—"the book of the origin of Jesus Christ, son of David, the son of Abraham" (1:1)—functions analogously to the formulae in 4:17 and 16:21, that is, it serves as introduction to the whole section of 1:2–4:16 where the "origin" of Jesus is described in order that the reader can have proper understanding of his person. Therefore, Kingsbury's outline of Matthew is complete:

I. 1:1–4:16 The Person of Jesus the Messiah
II. 4:17–16:20 The Proclamation of Jesus Messiah
III. 16:21–28:20 The Suffering, Death and Resurrection
        of Jesus Messiah

Whether this approach solves the question of Matthew's master-plan is debatable. Certainly Kingsbury's broad division of the Gospel does coincide with the major movements of Matthew's story, but did Matthew intend these specific time references as the linchpins of the whole structure? Matthew uses a similar phrase "$\alpha\pi o$ $\tau o\tau\epsilon$" ("from that time") in 26:16, where he describes Judas seeking an opportunity to betray Jesus. Kingsbury contends that this does not qualify because it is not a "fixed formula" such as 4:17 and 16:21 (From that time *Jesus began* . . ."). But do two uses in the entire Gospel enable one to label a phrase a "fixed formula"? And if Matthew wanted to give such importance to these two verses in his Gospel, is it likely that he would pen a very similar expression in 26:16? One can also question whether in 1:1 "the book of the origin" stands as a title for the entire section of 1:2–4:16, and also whether one can squeeze the thematic meaning of "person" from the term "genesis" or "origin" in 1:1.

New Ways of Posing the Question

Every "solution" to the question of Matthew's masterplan (and there are many more than the ones illustrated here) has some flaws. This has led some scholars to wonder if the question is being posed in the correct way. What exactly do we mean by "structure"? Should this be thought of as a detailed and comprehensive outline that the evangelist consciously designed beforehand and then proceeded to write his Gospel in rigid adherence to this blueprint? Such a scenario is not impossible, of course, but the failure of scholars to agree about this masterplan might suggest that Matthew did not proceed in such an orderly fashion.

Or does "plan" or "structure" mean something less comprehensive? Did Matthew, for instance, have a single idea or motif in mind as he sat down to compose his story, such as modeling the Gospel on the Pentateuch or on the Book of Deuteronomy or according to certain key phrases of Jesus' life? This approach, too, has its problems precisely because *each* motif suggested by scholars such as Bacon, Ellis, Frankemoëlle and Kingsbury has merit.

This might mean that Matthew's "plan" was, in fact, much less systematic and much richer in variety than most scholars have thought. A storyteller does not work in the same way as a mathematician. The storyteller does not usually begin with a rigid comprehensive plan. Instead the artistic mind of the narrator has some basic motifs he or she wants to express, some convictions about the characters who will people his or her story, and some idea of the basic plot or storyline. Only as the author begins to assemble the cast of characters and to spin out the story does the full structure emerge from what to that point may have been hunches and semi-conscious intuitions rather than a clear blueprint.

This type of composition process may, in fact, be closer to the procedure that shaped the plot or structure of Matthew's Gospel. After all, as recent exegesis has emphasized, the Gospels are stories and the evangelists are storytellers. In Matthew's case, some of the lines of that story were already fixed for him by his source, the Gospel of Mark. But Matthew had other sources and ideas he wanted to blend into his narrative. So his structure may best be described as a retelling of the story of Mark. He built his Gospel around the basic storyline provided by Mark (Jesus' public ministry in Galilee; a journey from Galilee to Jerusalem in the course of which Jesus predicts his passion and instructs his disciples; the final days in the Jerusalem temple and the climactic story of the passion and resurrection). But Matthew "retells" the story with his own touches, adding an infancy narrative, creating a ·series of discourses, extending the resurrection section to include appearances at the tomb and in Galilee, and so on. Even the materials he has taken over from Mark or Q are reshaped in Matthew's own style and perspective. The end result is a new telling of the traditional story of Jesus provided by Mark.

As Matthew moves the reader through his story there are several devices and motifs that carry the plot. The structure of the Gospel is more like the flowing lines of a symphony than the fixed girders supporting a building. Thus the great discourses with their concluding formulae and those key moments in the life of Jesus when he enters Galilee or sets out for Jerusalem (4:17 and 16:21) and the rising crescendo of opposition which breaks out in chapters 11–13 are all important movements in Matthew's on-going narrative. All of them together function as seams or turns within the Gospel's organic structure rather than as potential keys to a single fixed blueprint.

I have tried to follow this approach in my own commentary on Matthew.[17] And I hope the reader will indulge repeating my suggested outline here. Matthew's storyline encompasses the full span of Jesus life: I. (1:1–4:16) The origin of Jesus is traced in his birth and infancy and in his encounter with John (a place where Matthew joins up with Mark's story); II. (4:17–10:42) The pace quickens as Matthew unfolds Jesus' Galilean ministry, ordered around teaching (chapters 5–7) and healing (chapters 8–9), a ministry designed to serve as a model for the apostles' own mission (chapter 10); III. (11:1–16:20) A new phase of the story beings to emerge as Matthew shows varying responses to Jesus, both rejection by Jewish opponents and the glimmering faith of the disciples (note that Matthew follows the order of Mark's story much more closely from chapter 13 on); IV. (16:21–20:34) The drama of the death and resurrection of Jesus looms as Matthew follows Mark's lead and presents Jesus and his disciples on the way to Jerusalem; V. (21:1–28:15) The holy city is the center of focus where Jesus has his final days of teaching in the temple area, and when all his teaching is done (26:1), the passion story begins, leading to death and resurrection; VI. (28:16–20) The vivid finale (found only in Matthew) brings the Gospel story full term, back to Galilee where Jesus sends his disciples out into the world and promises his abiding presence.

Such a "structure" is, of course, not as thematically consistent or as architecturally symmetrical as some of the others we have sampled. But it does, I think, take into account the major movements of Matthew's story. A "structure" that gives attention to the nature of Matthew's Gospel as narrative, and therefore as a fluid, organic literary piece, has the best chance of taking into account the whole spectrum of Matthew's distinctive features.

3
Matthew's View
of Salvation History

Introduction

One of the major reasons Matthew wrote his Gospel was to give new perspective to a Christian community caught in the sweeping transition from a church mainly Jewish in character to one increasingly Gentile. This represents a strong consensus of contemporary scholarship, as we saw in our chapter on "The Setting for Matthew's Gospel."

It is not surprising, therefore, that Matthew should give special attention to history. He begins his Gospel story with a genealogy (1:2–18) that ties the life of Jesus back into the history of Israel, starting with Abraham, and moving through David and the time of the exile. Matthew constantly refers to the Old Testament, illustrating how Jesus "fulfilled" the promises given to Israel.[1] And Matthew's story ends with the risen Christ sending his apostles out on a mission that will take them not only to the ends of the earth, but to the end of time (28:20). Matthew's story, then, moves from the beginning to the end of sacred history.

This feature of the Gospel has also been a significant topic for current biblical research on Matthew. No student of the Gospel would deny that Matthew has a sense of "sacred" or "salvation history," but there is disagreement about how Matthew conceived of that history.

Since the term "salvation history" is somewhat vague and subject to many interpretations, it is wise to define what is meant at the outset. John Meier, in his book *The Vision of Matthew,* offers a good working definition:

> By salvation history we mean a schematic understanding of God's dealings with men that emphasizes continuity-yet-difference. Insofar as the theologian, reflecting on saving events, sees the one and the same God acting faithfully and consistently within the flow of time, he perceives continuity, a basic horizontal line (though not always a straight one). Insofar as the theologian sees the different ways in which God acts at different times and the different ways in which man responds, he perceives the lines of demarcation which delimit the distinct periods of this history—the vertical lines of division, as it were. Difference within continuity, the various stages within the one divine economy: this is the basic insight on which any outline or pattern of salvation history is built. (p. 30)

Salvation history, then, is a faith perspective; the believer looks back at the flow of historical events and detects a pattern which helps shape a religious consciousness of the present. Many of Matthew's fellow Christians may not have been able to see any continuity at all. They were cut off from their Jewish roots and facing an uncertain future with streams of Gentiles, along with their strange customs and ignorance of Judaism, now flowing into the church. By reflecting on "continuity-within-discontinuity," Matthew intended to give new perspective and therefore new hope to his baffled church.[2]

But exactly how did Matthew view this sacred or salvation history? What were its major turning points as it moved from Israel's past into the present of Matthew's church? To these questions contemporary Matthean scholars have given divergent answers.

A History in Three Stages

One of the earliest redaction critics to turn his attention exclusively to this question was Rolf Walker in his book *Die Heilsges-*

chichte im ersten Evangelium ("Salvation History in the First Gospel").[3] Walker builds a comprehensive schema that runs from Abraham on one end to the consummation of the world on the other. Along the way, according to Walker, Matthew's Gospel marks off key periods or stages in this sweep of sacred history.

The genealogy (1:1–18) shows that one major period runs from Abraham up to the birth of the Messiah Jesus. The messianic age itself is cast into two major periods. The first was the proclamation of the Gospel of the kingdom to Israel. This is evident, Walker suggests, in Matthew's narrative where Jesus restricts his mission to the house of Israel (see 10:5; 15:24). That period continued for the duration of the Church's mission to Israel up to A.D. 70 and the destruction of Jerusalem when the definitive failure of the Jewish mission became evident to Matthew's church. From that time on, a new and final period of history was in place: the mission to the Gentiles. This period, Walker argues, is signaled not only in the clear universal mission commission of 28:16–20 ("make disciples of all nations") but in Matthew's dual emphasis within the story of Jesus on Israel's rejection of Jesus and the favorable response of Gentiles (see for example, the centurion of 8:5–15, and the Canaanite woman of 15:21–28).

In other words, for Walker, the drama of the Gospel is a symbolic presentation of salvation history. The hostility between Jesus and the Jewish leaders is not reflective of a contemporary polemic between Matthew and Pharisaic Judaism but plays out the first stage of messianic salvation history. The leaders represent "Israel" which rejects the Messiah and sets the stage for a new period of sacred history in which the message of the kingdom is offered to Gentiles. This is the period in which Matthew's church finds itself. This, in Walker's view, helps ratify the Gentile mission and provides a way of understanding the tragic past.

Writing a bit earlier than Walker, George Strecker turned his attention to Matthew's historical perspective in an article entitled "Das Geschichtsverständnis des Matthäus" ("The Concept of History in Matthew").[4] Strecker notes "historicizing tendencies" in Matthew, not only in the addition of the genealogy and infancy narrative to Mark's storyline, but in other chronological references that reveal the evangelist's historical and chronological interest. For example, Matthew adds the phrase "from that time" at key moments of the Gospel story in 4:17; 16:21; 26:16.[5] Matthew also has geo-graphical allusions that Strecker considers part of the "historicizing tendency." For example, Matthew alone designates Capernaum as Jesus' "own city" (9:1) and refers to Jesus "dwelling" in Capernaum (9:13). For Mark, by contrast, references to houses are not fixed geo-graphically; they are merely settings in which Jesus' private instruc-tion to his disciples are given (see Mark 2:1; 3:20; 7:17; 9:28, 33; 10:10).

Other aspects of the Gospel reveal Matthew's interest in an his-torical perspective. Strecker appeals to the many Old Testament quo-tations which emphasize Jesus' fulfillment of the promises to Israel. In the infancy narrative these quotations are applied to the progres-sive stages of Jesus' own history: Bethlehem, Egypt, Nazareth, Ca-pernaum. The same is true for the references to the mission: during the lifetime of Jesus it is restricted to Israel (10:5–6; 15:24); only af-ter Jesus' death does it include Gentiles.

From this kind of evidence Strecker constructs what he believes is Matthew's view of salvation history. Sacred time has a three-stage progression: (I) *A time of preparation.* This encompasses the history of Israel prior to Jesus. The patriarchs and prophets point forward to Jesus; the fate of the prophets (cf. 23:29–39) foreshadows Jesus' own; (II) *The time of Jesus.* In this period Jesus and his message of the kingdom are directed exclusively to the people of Israel. This period comes to an end with the life of Jesus, including the rejection of his call to repentance and the consequent loss of Israel's priority within salvation history (cf. 21:43); (III) *The time of the Church.* This is a time of mission that is to last until the end of the world. This final age demands that the teaching of Jesus be carried out: it is to be a time of justice and obedience.

For Matthew, all of sacred history pivots around the life of Je-sus. Matthew thereby provides continuity for his community, but at the same time he is able to press his major interest which is ethical: full response to the words and deeds of Jesus in this climactic age which leads to the consummation of all history.

Both Walker and Strecker agree that the life of Jesus is central to Matthew's salvation history perspective. But the two authors part ways on which events flag key moments in the schema. For Walker, the failure of the mission to Israel and the opening to the Gentiles—

events which take definite shape around the watershed date of A.D.
70—are the turning point. Matthew's "life of Jesus" is told in such a
way that it reflects these later realities. Strecker, on the other hand,
gives more emphasis to the past reality of Jesus' life. His historical
existence is the turning point between the past of Israel and the present of the Church.

Death–Resurrection as Turning Point

A more recent study of the question is that of John Meier. First
in an article entitled "Salvation History in Matthew: In Search of a
Starting Point," and later in his doctoral dissertation *Law and History in Matthew's Gospel,* and in his book on Matthew's theology entitled *The Vision of Matthew* (a distillation of his thesis), Meier
wrestles with this issue.[6]

Meier does not attempt to sketch out the full spectrum of sacred
history as Walker and Strecker had done; instead, he concentrates on
the events of Jesus' life as presented by Matthew. He contends that it
is not just the "life of Jesus" as such which represents the turning
point of history for Matthew, but specifically the death and resurrection of Jesus. When Matthew describes the events that surround the
moment of Jesus' death, he does so in a way that clearly signals his
interpretation of these events (see 27:51–54): the temple veil is torn
in two, and there is an earthquake, a shattering of the tombs and the
triumphant raising of the holy ones of Israel from the dead. The tear-
ing of the temple veil as a sign of God's judgment on the old dispen-
sation is already present in Mark's Gospel (Mk. 15:38). But the
earthquake and the resurrection of the dead are added by Matthew.
These kinds of dramatic events are also found in apocalyptic writings
of Judaism, such as the Book of Enoch, written roughly contemporary with Matthew. These were considered typical signs of the final
age, the coming of the great day of the Lord when, as Meier notes,
"Death is vanquished and must yield up its captives."[7] Matthew may
have been inspired by the vision of Ezekiel 37:1–14 (especially vv. 7,
12–14) which presents new life coming to the dead bones of Israel.
This passage apparently had special meaning for the Judaism of Matthew's era.[8]

Meier also notes that the finale of Matthew's death scene is the acclamation of Jesus by the centurion and his companions (27:54): "Indeed he was the Son of God." Therefore, Matthew presents the death (and ultimate victory) of Jesus as a decisive moment in sacred history: the old age symbolized by the temple is over, a new age of resurrection has begun, and the Gentiles are beginning to respond to Jesus.

The death scene in 27:51–54 is not the only place Matthew uses this kind of imagery. He follows through in his narration of the empty tomb story by enriching the account of his source Mark with more apocalyptic descriptions. As the women are coming to see the tomb, there is a "great earthquake," and a fearsome "angel of the Lord" with a radiant appearance causes the guards to fall into a tremor (28:2–4). These details, too, are similar to the way Jewish literature described the expected events of the final age (see, for example, Daniel 7:9; 10:5–6; 10:8, 16).

Meier believes that these passages help us interpret how Matthew viewed salvation history. The evangelist presents not just the life of Jesus in general as a turning point in salvation history but the very climax of his redemptive mission—death and resurrection—as the hinge on which the history turns. This helps fit into place other pieces of Matthew's narrative. The concluding passage of 28:16–20 where the risen Christ appears to his disciples on a Galilean mountain top and sends them out on a worldwide mission is a "proleptic parousia."[9] Matthew uses this scene to show Jesus as the Son of Man coming in triumph to his Church, a foretaste of the final coming which will take place at the definitive consummation of history. But even now, Matthew's Gospel insists, that triumphant parousia of the Lord is present in the Church.

This view of history enables us in turn to understand how Matthew handled other issues of his Gospel. Prior to the death and resurrection of Jesus, the mission is restricted to Israel (see 10:5–6; 15:24), but when the new age begins at the cross the mission can become universal (28:16–20). Prior to the new age the Jewish law was in effect (5:18), but with the coming of a "new heavens and a new earth" through the events of death–resurrection, that old law is replaced by the Torah of Jesus.[10]

Matthew, then, attempted to give perspective to some of the radical changes his community was experiencing by reminding them that the death and resurrection of Jesus had triggered the final age of salvation for which Israel longed. In this new age dramatic transformations were to take place.

A Two-Stage History

Another author who has given careful attention to Matthew's view of salvation history is Jack Dean Kingsbury in his book *Matthew: Structure, Christology, Kingdom*.[11] He reviews the opinions of some of the authors we have considered and notes that most of them come up with a "three-epoch" division of salvation history: (1) Israel, (2) the life of Jesus, (3) the time of the Church, even though there are some variations on the precise demarcations of each period. Kingsbury also notes that for each of these authors the basis of division is some ecclesial concern. For Walker, it is the beginning of the Gentile mission; for Strecker it is ethical concerns; for Meier it is the abrogation of law and the shift in the Church's mission.

Kingsbury himself goes in another direction. He believes that Matthew has only a "two-epoch" division of salvation history: (1) a time of Israel which is "preparatory to and prophetic of the coming of the Messiah" and (2) the time of Jesus "in which the time of Israel finds its fulfillment and which, from the vantage point of Matthew's day, extends from the beginning of the ministry of John and Jesus (past) through the post-Easter time (present) to the coming consummation of the age (future)" (p. 31). Kingsbury believes that Matthew has constructed his two-stage schema of salvation history not on ecclesial grounds but on the basis of Christology.

To support his thesis, Kingsbury points to evidence in the Gospel which shows that Matthew considered his community to be in essential continuity with the period begun with the advent of Jesus. What is constitutive of this period of salvation history is the abiding presence of Jesus. Matthew affirms this at the very beginning of the Gospel where Jesus is named "Emmanuel—God-with-us" (1:23), as well as at the end when the risen Christ promises his continual presence with his apostles (28:20). This shows that the "time of Jesus" extends "from his birth to the parousia" (p. 31).

Other features of Matthew bolster this schema, according to Kingsbury. The time of the Church is only a "substage" of the time of Jesus, not a separate epoch. In contrast to Luke, Matthew has no ascension account nor does he have a developed theology of the Spirit. This is because for Matthew the risen Jesus continues to abide in the Church (see 13:37–38; 18:20; 28:18–20). This is also reflected in the exalted character of Jesus as portrayed in Matthew. The Matthean Jesus is "worshiped" (14:33) and consistently addressed by the disciples as "Lord." In the same vein Matthew portrays the disciples as more "understanding" of Jesus (13:1, 16, 51) and as knowing and doing the will of the Father (12:49–50). All of this, in Kingsbury's view, shows that Matthew saw essential continuity between the time of Jesus and the time of the Church. In the evangelist's schema, the decisive element is his Christology. The person of Jesus, earthly and exalted, has triggered a new and final age of salvation history, an age in which Matthew's church participates because of the abiding presence of the risen Lord in the midst of the community of faith.

Conclusion

As with the question of structure, so here it may be that Matthew's own concept of salvation history was not as clear or consistent as biblical scholars would prefer. Did Matthew define his schema so precisely that he could decide whether his fundamental rationale was Christological or ecclesiological? And could Matthew tell us whether his distinction between the time of Jesus and the time of the Church formed two distinctive stages or merely that of "sub-categories" within one stage?

Perhaps for Matthew *all* of the important features singled out by modern interpreters were in play at once. He was guided by ecclesial concerns *and* by his Christological convictions. He saw both continuity *and* separation between the life of Jesus and the time of the Church. What is sure is that Matthew was trying to tie the present situation of his Christians into the broad sweep of on-going salvation history. That history found its origin and its promise in Israel. The person and mission of Jesus, particularly his death and resurrection, had brought that sacred history to a decisive new moment. The Christian faith of Matthew's community had led to radical changes:

isolation from the synagogue, an influx of Gentiles, radical adaptation of the traditional Jewish law, harassment from both Roman and Jewish authorities, tensions and divisions within the community.

By recalling the flow of history, Matthew reminded his church that such tribulations were not death rattles but the birth pangs of the new age inaugurated by Jesus, an age in which death would ultimately be overcome. Allegiance to Jesus the Messiah meant not just radical changes but new life and new hope. His mission in which the community shared and his healing presence in their midst fulfilled the dreams of Israel and thus provided deep continuity with the past and energetic hope for the future.

If the precise details of Matthews historical perspective remain debatable, the overall thrust of his perspective and its pastoral purpose are clear.

4
Matthew's Use of the Old Testament

Introduction

Any careful reader of Matthew's Gospel is struck by the way the evangelist appeals to the Old Testament. Matthew connects numerous events of Jesus' life with specific passages from the Hebrew Scriptures. Besides these obvious quotations Matthew's story is full of imagery and subtle allusions from the Old Testament.

The Fulfillment Quotations

Recent studies of Matthew have turned their microscope on this aspect of the Gospel, too. The most intriguing texts are the so-called "formula" or "fulfillment" quotations. These are the eleven (or twelve by some counts) quotations from the Old Testament introduced by a stereotype formula stressing the idea of fulfillment and applied to specific events or aspects of Jesus' life.[1] Since these quotations are a unique feature of Matthew's Gospel, scholars believe that this material can give us some information about the origin and purpose of Matthew's narrative.

The fulfillment quotations span the entire Gospel, covering the events of Jesus' birth (1:23; 2:6, 15, 18, 23), his entry into Galilee (4:15–16), his healings (8:17), his compassion and gentleness (12:18–21), his teaching in parables (13:35), his entry into Jerusalem (21:5), his passion and death (26:56; 27:9–10). But even though the full spectrum of the Gospel is touched, most of the fulfillment quotations are limited to the first thirteen chapters and especially to those passages that are most uniquely Matthean such as the infancy narratives of chapters 1 and 2. Note, too, that many of the quotations are from the prophets.

All of these characteristics feed into the current discussion of the fulfillment quotations. Three major questions stand out: (1) What is the text form of the quotations? In other words, did Matthew draw these quotations from the Hebrew Bible (thus showing his knowledge of Hebrew) and, if so, what version? Or did he use the Septuagint, the ancient Greek translation of the Old Testament favored by the Greek-speaking early church? Or did Matthew make his own translation? This issue can be decided, of course, only by a careful comparison of the Greek text of Matthew with the many editions of the Hebrew Bible and Septuagint known to us today. (2) A second question is that of the "origin" of these quotations. Did the evangelist himself select and shape them as he wrote his Gospel? Or were they already a collection of Old Testament texts that had been applied to Jesus by the early Church? Or did they have some other origin such as a collection of texts for use in preaching? (3) A final major issue has to do with the purpose of the quotations. Did Matthew incorporate them to prove that Jesus was the Messiah? Or to counteract Jewish arguments against Jesus? Or is there a more positive theological purpose to their presence in the Gospel?

To illustrate some of the answers that modern biblical scholarship has given to these questions we will sample the views of three Matthean interpreters who come to some very different conclusions.

The School of Saint Matthew

One of the first major studies of this question in recent decades was that of Krister Stendahl, *The School of St. Matthew and Its Use of the Old Testament,* originally published in 1954 and appearing in a second edition in 1968.[2]

Stendahl's basic goal was to study the Old Testament quotations in Matthew, but he placed that question in the broader context of a hypothesis about the setting in which Matthew's Gospel was produced. He stresses many of those features that distinguish Matthew: its ordered structure, with the inclusion of extensive discourse material, its concern with church leadership (16:16 and chapter 18) and church discipline (18:15–20), and its studied use of Old Testament quotations. In Stendahl's view these elements give Matthew's Gospel the character of a "handbook" for church life. Such a "handbook" would be the product of a "school," that is, a loosely organized "milieu of study and instruction" (p. 29). It was a "school for teachers and church leaders" with the Gospel assuming the form of a manual for teachers and administrators within the church (p. 35). Such a school has analogies in rabbinic circles but Stendahl believed that the closest parallel may have been Qumran, the monastic center of strict Judaism that developed on the shores of the Dead Sea from 132 B.C. to A.D. 70. This brotherhood of Jews "acted as a school which preserved and expounded the doctrines and rules of its founder" (p. 31).

Stendahl contends that the "crown jewel" of Matthew's "school" was its use of the Old Testament to interpret the life of Jesus. In fact, this may be the closest affinity between Qumran and the school of Matthew: the way the Qumran group interpreted the Old Testament Book of Habakkuk is similar in style to the way Matthew handled Old Testament quotations. For Qumran, as for Matthew, the Old Testament texts were not primarily a source of rules "but the prophecy which was shown to be fulfilled" for both the Founder and his followers (p. 35).

Stendahl attempts to demonstrate his thesis by a detailed study of Old Testament quotations in Matthew. He finds that in those texts which Matthew has in common with Mark and Luke the form is similar to that of the Septuagint, or Greek Bible. But in the fulfillment texts, or what Stendahl called the "formula quotations," the text form, although composed in Greek, is closer to the Masoretic or standard Hebrew text while showing "deviations from all Greek, Hebrew and Aramaic types of texts known to us" (p. 97). Stendahl attributes this to the creative work of Matthew and his school. "In the distinction from the rest of the Synoptics and the Epistles with what seems to be their self-evident use of the LXX (Septuagint), Matthew was capable of having, and did have, the authority to create a rendering of his own" (p. 127).

The analogy to Qumran helped Stendahl explain this peculiarity of Matthew. The Qumran group applied quotations from the Book of Habbakuk to their founder, "The Teacher of Righteousness"; they were convinced that these prophecies found their fulfillment and their ultimate meaning in this person and the community he founded. The quotations they used from the Book of Habbakuk are a unique form, indicating that the Qumran group felt free to adapt and shape the text in the light of their convictions about its fulfillment.[3] This type of *pesher* method (from the Hebrew and Aramaic word meaning "interpretation") is what Matthew and his school exercised with the formula quotations. Because they were convinced that Jesus was the fulfillment of the Messianic prophecies of the Old Testament, Matthew's school shaped and rendered these key quotations to fit the contours of their traditions about Jesus and his teaching. Thus the formula quotations, according to Stendahl, not only lead us to the strong fulfillment Christology of Matthew but also give us an insight into the structure of Matthew's community.

Notetaker for Jesus

While Stendahl's basic thesis about a school setting for Matthew's Gospel has not been widely accepted, his detailed examination of the text form of Matthew's quotations continues to be a valuable resource. More recent studies have gone in other directions. One of the most unusual is the work of Robert Gundry, *The Use of the Old Testament in St. Matthew's Gospel, With Special Reference to the Messianic Hope.*[4]

Gundry studied not only explicit quotations of the Old Testament in Matthew but even more subtle allusions (an example would be the allusion to Isaiah 63:19 in Matthew 3:16 where there is reference to the "opening of the heavens"). He agrees with Stendahl that such a free form is found only in Matthew's fulfillment quotations. The quotations Matthew shares with Mark are based on the Septuagint but all other quotations and allusions in the Synoptic materials have evidence of the same kind of "mixed form" as that in the fulfillment quotations.

This leads Gundry to further challenge Stendahl's theory about a special Matthean school as the source of the supposedly unique Old Testament quotations Matthew used. Gundry insists that the practice of making one's own translation of Old Testament materials— rather than depending on the Masoretic text or the Septuagint—was more common in the early Church than one may have supposed. The Jewish Christians were, after all, used to the rabbinic practice of "targumizing," that is, of free, interpretive renderings of biblical quotations and stories. But Gundry pushes his case much further. He suggests that the mixture of Hebrew, Septuagintal (i.e., Greek) and Aramaic elements in Matthew's quotations "harmonizes perfectly" with what we know of the trilingual milieu of Palestine in the first century. The only adequate explanation is that the source of these quotations is ultimately Matthew the apostle. Matthew, an educated publican, would be equipped for this role. He may, in fact, have been a "notetaker" among the band of Jesus' disciples, recording events and discourses of Jesus, even the interpretation of the Old Testament that Jesus applied to himself and to his messianic mission. These notes, according to Gundry, would have been the foundation of the tradition upon which the Synoptic Gospels were built. Gundry holds that the Gospel of Matthew depended directly on the Greek Gospel of Mark (this accounts for the presence of Septuagintal Old Testament quotations which Matthew brought over from Mark) but the ultimate source was the raw material provided by the tax collector Matthew. Thus Gundry envisages a very early date for Mark and Matthew, somewhere around A.D. 50–60.[5]

The theological meaning of the Old Testament quotations in Matthew is also of importance for Gundry's study. Gundry synthesizes Matthew's theology under the label "messianic hope." Matthew's Old Testament quotations cover a broad spectrum of Israel's hopes for salvation. Each set of quotations and allusions draws on these basic images of hope: Jesus is the royal Messiah, the Isaian Servant, the Danielic Son of Man, the Shepherd of Israel; he fulfills the role of Yahweh himself in saving from sin (1:21), raising the dead (11:5) and giving rest to the weary (11:28–29). He is the greater Moses, the greater Son of David, the representative prophet like Jeremiah and Elisha; he is the representative Israelite and the true just sufferer of Israel.

Thus, by means of Old Testament quotations and allusions, a wide spectrum of messianic images and types find their fulfillment in Jesus. This interpretation, Gundry believes, was not merely the post-Easter reflection of the Church. The validation for that reflection was Jesus' own intepretation of the Scriptures in the light of his mission. This interpretation was faithfully transmitted by Matthew's notes.

The Fulfillment Texts and the Plan of Matthew's Gospel

The studies of Stendahl and Gundry concentrated mainly on the form and origin of the fulfillment quotations used by Matthew. The important work of Wilhelm Rothfuchs, *Die Erfüllungszitate des Matthäus-Evangeliums* ("The Fulfillment Quotations of Matthew's Gospel") tries to appreciate how these quotations fit into Matthew's theology.[6] In many ways, Rothfuchs' book demonstrates the kind of contribution that redaction criticism adds to methods of historical and form criticism.

Rothfuchs agrees that the text form of the quotations is mixed, a blend of Septuagintal elements with unique translations. But he disagrees with the theory of Stendahl that these came from the exegetical work of a school. He also challenges the proposal of Georg Strecker that these quotations were part of a collection (or "testimonial") of Old Testament quotations used in the early Church to prove Jesus' messianic identity. Strecker claimed that the citations in Matthew did not really reflect the evangelist's style, and the quotations give the impression of being forced into the text without an intrinsic relationship to the surrounding context. For example, the quotation from 2 Chronicles 29:30 in Matthew 13:35 speaks of *revelation:* "I will open my mouth in parables. I will utter what has been hidden since the foundation of the world." Yet, Strecker points out, Matthew uses the term "parable" in a negative sense in this chapter, as a vehicle not of revelation but of concealment for those who reject Jesus: "This is why I speak to them in parables, because seeing they do not see, and hearing they do not hear, nor do they understand" (13:13). This shows that the formula quotation is out of step with its context and was imported by the evangelist from a pre-existing collection of quotations. The only function of the Old Testament quotations for Matthew is to stress the "fact" of Jesus' life; the citations are part of a historicizing tendency in Matthew.[7]

But Rothfuchs disagrees on almost all counts. He insists that a careful study of the form of the quotations and their introductory formulae show that they are integrated with the evangelist's style and perspective, and that their purpose is more theological than Strecker thinks.

One factor to keep in mind is the context in which these quotations appear. In the case of Matthew 13:35, for example, it is true that the parables are referred to as veiled speech for those who reject Jesus. But more of the context has to be taken into account. A turning point in the chapter occurs in 13:36, immediately after the Old Testament quotation: Jesus leaves the crowd and teaches the disciples privately in a house. According to Rothfuchs and others,[8] this divides the discourse and, in fact, is a watershed for the whole Gospel story. Prior to 13:36 Jesus had spoken to all of Israel and, especially beginning with chapter 11, had experienced misunderstanding and rejection. From now on his mission is turned away from his opponents to the community of the disciples who do understand (13:11, 16, 51).

The fulfillment quotation accurately reflects this Matthean perspective. It is placed not at the end of the discourse but at the turning point after v. 34. Its content echoes the movement of the whole discourse: the first part, "I will open my mouth in parables," parallels the first half of the chapter in which Jesus directed parables to the crowds; the second half, "I will utter what has been hidden since the foundation of the world," coincides with the special revelation of the mystery of the kingdom which is given to the disciples and signaled in the second half of the discourse. Therefore, as this example shows, the fulfillment quotations are not bootlegged from some pre-existing source but were carefully integrated into the Gospel by the evangelist.

Rothfuchs applies his redaction criticism method not just to individual occurrences of the quotations but to their distribution in the Gospel as a whole. He notes that with the exception of 27:9–10 (the death of Judas) and 21:4–5 (entry into Jerusalem) the fulfillment texts are bunched in the infancy narrative of chapters 1 and 2 or, with the four quotes attributed to Isaiah, applied to Jesus' public ministry in Galilee (4:14–15; 8:17; 12:18–21; 13:35). These quotations, especially the Isaian ones, apply to Jesus' mission to the lost sheep of the house of Israel. Jesus carries out God's promised mission of salvation to his people.

This gives Rothfuchs a hint as to the origin of this style of Old Testament interpretation. It developed in the missionary preaching of the early Church's mission to Israel.[9] The Church's basic message to the Jews was that the promises were fulfilled in Jesus. But the mission to Israel had become a thing of the past by the time Matthew writes his Gospel; now the mission is turned toward the Gentiles (28:16–20). So Matthew's Old Testament interpretation has a new purpose. Now it is the message of the community that the promises of salvation made to Israel and fulfilled in Jesus are, through his risen presence in the Church, available to all people. This universal perspective is reflected not only in the explicit mission text of 28:16–20 but in the content of some of the Old Testament quotations themselves (see 12:17 with its quotation of Is. 42:1–4).

Conclusion

Each of these authors has offered different answers to the three questions posed at the beginning of the chapter about the form, origin and purpose of the fulfillment quotations. But the state of the art on this question is not pure anarchy. An article by the Flemish scholar Frans Van Segbroeck helps bring some synthesis to this issue.[10] His observations can serve as a conclusion to our review.

I. *The Form.* Van Segbroeck finds a good bit of consensus here. The thesis of Stendahl and many others that the fulfillment quotations are a mixed text form blending LXX, Hebrew and Aramaic elements has been sustained. Gundry has gone further, asserting that this mixed form is probably true of many other citations of the Old Testament in the Gospels. What makes the Old Testament fulfillment quotations in Matthew's Gospel unique is not the textual form but the way the evangelist applies these quotations to the life of Jesus. The authors also seem to agree that Matthew's quotations were formulated in Greek, thus indicating a Hellenistic church, one in close contact with its Jewish roots.

II. *The Origin.* Consensus is not as strong here. The "school" theory of Stendahl has not been widely accepted, nor has the conservative view of Gundry that these come from the original notes of Matthew. Gundry's thesis also places the Gospel of Matthew too early and compresses too radically the time span it would take for

Mark's Gospel to be formulated and for Matthew to be able to revise this Gospel in his own format. Many scholars also believe that Matthew's Gospel shows signs of being aware of the destruction of Jerusalem in A.D. 70, and of the Jamnia reform, and therefore must be dated much later than Gundry suggests.[11]

Strecker's theory that the quotations were part of a collection or testimonial has not been given a warm reception either. Ironically, the discovery of the Dead Sea Scrolls proved that such collections were known in Judaism; prior to that archeological find the existence of such collections was merely a hypothesis. But most scholars are still not convinced that Matthew drew his quotations from such a source.

More weight seems to be given to the "preaching" milieu suggested by Kilpatrick and refined by Rothfuchs. "Preaching" must be understood in a broad sense to include all of the teaching and communication activities of the Church's mission. In this context the early Church probably developed a style of applying key Old Testament texts, especially from the prophets and psalms, to the events of Jesus' life, illustrating that he was the fulfillment of Israel's hopes. This process may have begun in the passion story but was soon applied to all of the events of Jesus' life.

This tradition of Old Testament interpretation, developed in the course of the Church's mission among Jews, may well have been the origin of the style of interpretation found in Matthew's Gospel.

III. *The Meaning.* Van Segbroeck observes that more work now needs to be done in this area. Rothfuchs' book is one of the few major studies from an explicitly redactional perspective. Rothfuchs does not go far enough, in Van Segbroeck's view. For example, the rationale behind the distribution of the Old Testament quotations in the Gospel might be discovered by realizing that chapters 1–13, where most of them occur, are precisely those passages where Matthew takes the freest hand vis-à-vis his source, Mark.[12] This reinforces the suggestion that the quotations are specifically Matthean and are important to his perspective. Van Segbroeck also suggests that the attribution of so many of the quotations to Isaiah is significant. Not only was Isaiah the premier messenger of salvation to Israel (a point made by Rothfuchs) but he was also the prophet who most bemoaned the *failure* of his mission. This, too, might be a reason for Matthew's use of texts from that prophet, since much of his Gospel wrestles with Israel's rejection of Jesus and the Christian mission.

The contribution of redaction critics such as Rothfuchs and Van Segbroeck is to show that the Old Testament quotations in Matthew are not mere "proof texts" or embroideries on the Gospel story but an integral part of the Gospel's message. The quotations highlight almost every aspect of Jesus and his mission—his origin, his ministry of the kingdom, his miracles, his teaching, his advent in Israel and in the holy city Jerusalem, his rejection, suffering and death. In all of this, God's promises of salvation were taking flesh, and this conviction—proclaimed in concert with the Hebrew Scriptures—is what Matthew's Gospel wished to proclaim.

5
Matthew's Attitude to the Law

Introduction

No single facet of Matthew's theology stands on its own. That is certainly true of Matthew's attitude to the Jewish law, another focal point of current scholarship. How the Gospel understands the role of the law is closely related to many of the questions we have already considered: the evangelist's milieu, his perspective on salvation history, his use of the Old Testament. The law question also catapults us into the areas of Christology and Church, chapters yet to come.

It is important at the outset to state what is meant by "law" in this discussion. It refers primarily to the Jewish "law," that is, to the Torah or Pentateuch that functioned as the revealed word of God, and therefore as primary religious norm for Israel's life. But the law issue extends beyond this to include Matthew's reactions to the *interpretation* of the law as reflected in Pharisaic or other Jewish traditions. As we will see, the problem posed for Matthew's community was not so much the validity or value of the Torah as such, but the Torah as interpreted in the light of Jesus' own teachings.

There are many reasons why the issue of the law is a major question in current studies on Matthew's Gospel. One non-biblical reason is that the role of law in Christian life has always been problematical, especially for Protestant traditions. Some studies of Matthew take this contemporary issue as their point of departure.[1] But it is clear from the Gospel itself that the law was an important concern for Matthew and his church. In a much discussed text unique to

Matthew, Jesus states: "Think not that I have come to abolish the law and the prophets: I have come not to abolish them but to fulfill them" (5:17). A large portion of the Sermon on the Mount is taken up with interpretation of law (5:17–48). Controversies between Jesus and his opponents about questions of the law abound in the Gospel (see, for example, 9:1–8, 9–13, 14–17; 12:1–8, 9–14; 15:1–20; 17:24–27; 19:3–9; 22:15–22, 23–33, 34–40); in some instances, Matthew will even alter a story from his source Mark, making it into a conflict over law (compare, for example, Matthew 22:34–40 with Mark 12:28–34). The biting invective of chapter 23 seems directed against the law interpretation of the "scribes and Pharisees."

There is no question, then, that the Jewish law and its interpretation was an important issue for Matthew. The problem is to determine precisely what Matthew's views on the law are. Some texts of the Gospel seem to move in different directions. The Matthean Jesus is intent on fulfilling the law (5:17) and commands fidelity to "every 'iota' and 'dot' " (5:18–19), but in the same discourse important provisions of the Jewish law such as taking oaths, the law of talion and divorce seem to be overthrown (5:31–32, 33–37, 38–42).[2] The scribes and Pharisees are excoriated for their interpretation of the law, yet their authority seems to be upheld (23:2–3). The Matthean Jesus seems to freely bend or interpret the law to the priorities of his ministry (e.g., 12:1–8), yet he also lashes out at "lawless" ones within the community (7:23; 13:41; 24:12; in each instance the word *anomia* or "lawless," sometimes translated as "evildoers," is used) and constant emphasis is placed on the importance of good deeds.

Trying to fit these apparently divergent viewpoints into a coherent theological perspective has been an on-going struggle in Matthean scholarship. We will sample some of the solutions offered.

The "Two-Front" Theory

One of the first major redactional studies of Matthew's attitude to the law was that of Gerhard Barth in his contribution to the important book, *Tradition and Interpretation in Matthew.*[3] His long essay of over one hundred pages is entitled "Matthew's Understanding of the Law."

The heart of Barth's thesis is that Matthew's attitude to the law gains coherence when it is seen in the context of the evangelist's milieu. Barth suggests that Matthew was carrying on a struggle on two fronts. One group was the "antinomians," Christians who dismissed the law; against them Matthew stressed the enduring validity of the law, emphasized the need for good deeds, and raised the threat of judgment. On the other front were the rabbis of Pharisaic Judaism; against their interpretation of law Matthew stressed the priority of the love command and Jesus' own radicalizing of the law.[4]

Barth admits that attempts to identify precisely the "antinomians" are doomed to frustration. They were a group of Christians who apparently maintained that Christ had abolished the law and the prophets. To counteract this, Matthew stressed that Jesus did not come to abolish the law (5:17). These antinomians seem to have relied on their charismatic gifts of prophecy and miracle working (see 7:21–22) as sufficient proof of their righteousness, but Matthew countered this with an emphasis on good deeds and action in accord with Jesus' teaching as the only criterion for judgment (7:21–27). Barth speculates that this group was composed of Hellenistic Christians since it is unlikely that Jewish Christians would dismiss the law entirely, and we do have indications of charismatic activity in the Gentile church.[5] However, Barth did not believe that Matthew was pitted against a Pauline group (as might be the case in James). Beyond this Barth was not willing to speculate.

Matthew's other front against the rabbis kept the Gospel from becoming merely another version of Pharisaic tradition. While Matthew emphasizes that Jesus affirmed the validity of the law, the evangelist stands in opposition to Pharisaic *interpretation* of the law. As so many of the controversial stories of the Gospel illustrate—particularly the debate in 22:34–40—the absolute primacy of the love command is seen as the distinctive emphasis of Jesus' mission. This, claims Barth, puts Jesus' teaching in opposition to the interpretation of Pharisaic Judaism because the rabbis, in principle, claimed that each demand of the law is as important as the rest. By making the love command the fundamental principle of interpretation for all of the law (22:40), Matthew's Gospel parted company with the Pharisaic understanding of law. In this, Barth suggests, Matthew was faithfully reflecting the sayings of Jesus and Christian tradition, but no other Gospel writer expressed the issue so forthrightly.

Matthew: Moderator of Traditions

Written in 1972, R. Hammerton-Kelly's article, "Attitudes to the Law in Matthew's Gospel: A Discussion of Matthew 5:18," links the law question with the turbulent years of the late 1960's.[6] Does law have a place in a Christian context? The author suggests that Matthew's Gospel may offer some guidelines.

Matthew's perspective on the law is shaped not by opposition to antinomian Christians and Pharisees but by the attempt to moderate polarities in attitudes to the law within the Christian community itself. Hammerton-Kelly detects in the Gospel three different viewpoints: (1) a legally rigorous attitude which insisted that the law of Moses continued to be valid with all its force; (2) a view (probably similar to Stephen's Hellenists in the Book of Acts) which held that some of the law had been abrogated by Jesus, especially those parts which inhibited the mission to the Gentiles; (3) a view which held that the law was valid but that the authority of the traditional *halacha* or interpretation of the law had been replaced by the authority of the risen Christ.

It was the third view that Matthew himself espoused. The key issue, Hammerton-Kelly suggests, was not whether the law could be interpreted—this was already done in Judaism—but by what authority it would be so done. Thus the law issue is firmly linked to Christology. Hammerton-Kelly finds the justification of his position in the key passage 5:17–19, especially 5:18: "For truly, I say to you, till heaven and earth pass away, not an iota, not a dot, will pass from the law until all is accomplished." Here one can witness the combination and interaction of the various viewpoints expressed above. The text of 5:17–18 down to but excluding the final phrase of v. 18 "until all is accomplished" represents the rigorist attitude. The addition of this final phrase exercised a moderating influence on the original text. "Until all things are accomplished" refers, in Hammerton-Kelley's view, to the resurrection of Jesus, the turning point in salvation history whereby the authority of the risen Christ supplants that of previous interpretations of law. This juncture enables Matthew to add the antitheses of 5:21–48 which, in fact, radically went beyond traditional understanding of the law. This new "righteousness (5:20) represents Jesus' teaching on the law. The law remains valid, but only the law as filtered through the teaching authority of the risen Christ. Therefore, concludes Hammerton-Kelly, Matthew's perspective on law was a moderate position, in between the rigorous Jewish-Christian conservatives and the ultra-liberal Hellenists.

Two points made by Hammerton-Kelly have been amplified in other full-length studies of the law question.[7] First of all, the apparently divergent viewpoints in the Gospel are accounted for by layers of tradition; for example, earlier more stringent views on the law's validity are included in the Gospel but modified by Matthew's own more moderate perspective. Secondly, Hammerton-Kelly locates Matthew's theological perspective on the level of Christology and salvation history. Jesus' authority as the risen Christ underwrites a new interpretation of the function and even the content of the Torah.

Before turning to further illustrations of this perspective, however, we need to consider another viewpoint.

A New Law

The classical stance of B. Bacon and others who viewed the structure and theological perspective of Matthew as a "New Pen-teuch" had important consequences for their view of the law. Since Jesus was depicted as the new Moses, his Sermon on the Mount was considered the establishment of a new Torah, replacing the now invalid law of the former covenant. Jesus' famous statement about "fulfilling" rather than abolishing the "law" (5:17) meant that his new law fulfilled and effectively replaced the old. The stringent sayings of 5:18–19 about observing the least commandment and respecting every iota apply not to the Jewish law but to the newly established Torah of Jesus.

This viewpoint and the conception of Matthew's Gospel on which it is based have not received much support in recent scholarship. Few contemporary interpreters believe that the complexities of Matthew's theology can be adequately expressed by depicting Jesus simply as the "new Moses" or the new messianic "lawgiver."

However, the emphasis on the disjuncture between Jesus' teaching and the Jewish law has found some support in recent studies. A good example is that of Robert Banks in his article, "Matthew's Understanding of the Law: Authenticity and Interpretation in Matthew 5:17–20."[8] Banks does not agree with Bacon's Pentateuchal theory and his interpretation of Matthew's attitude to the law is subtly expressed, but, in the final analysis, Banks subordinates the law's perduring validity to the new authority of the risen Christ.

An important element in Banks' position is the meaning of the term *plēroun* ("fulfill") in Matthew 5:17.[9] He argues that the meaning of the verb in literature roughly contemporary with Matthew suggests that *plēroun* does not simply mean to "realize" or "establish" or "complete." The most frequent and revealing use of the term was in connection with the fulfillment of Old Testament prophecy. Therefore, it means not only realization or "actualization" but has a further nuance of "newness" or "superiority." It is this range of meaning that best expresses Matthew's phrase, "to fulfill the law and the prophets," in 5:17. There is an element of continuity (the law pointed prophetically to Jesus), but also of discontinuity ("that which is more than the law has now been realized"). This attitude to the law, Banks contends, is also expressed in the antitheses of 5:21–48, where Jesus' teaching moves beyond the law.

Banks concludes that for Matthew the Mosaic law had a "prophetic and so provisional function" (p. 242). Matthew was concerned to depict not so much Jesus' stance toward the law but "how the law stands with regard to him, as one who brings it to fulfillment and to whom all attention must now be directed" (p. 242). Such a position, of course, would put Matthew on a collision course with Pharisaic Judaism.

Law and the Total Context of Matthew

We can conclude our discussion with two major studies on the law question that have appeared in the past decade. Both exemplify the best of redaction critical methodology and both attempt to synthesize Matthew's position on the law with the total context of the Gospel.

Alexander Sand's book is entitled *Das Gesetz und die Propheten* ("The Law and the Prophets"); its subtitle, "Investigation of the Theology of the Gospel according to Matthew," indicates his broad scope.[10] Sand's thesis attempts to account for the subtlety of Matthew's viewpoint on the law and, especially, to relate it to the practical "ethical" concerns of the evangelist.

On a most basic level, Matthew means by "law" the Torah of the Old Testament both in its character as revealed word of God to his elect people Israel and as the norm and regulation for their life. It encompasses, in this most basic sense, the totality of the "handed on and written revelation of God." For Matthew the Torah in this sense remains valid; Jesus does not destroy it but fulfills it, that is, in the preaching of Jesus the will of God revealed in the law is freshly and definitively expressed (5:17). Matthew presents Jesus' attacks on the Jewish leaders not as questions about the validity of the law but as in the line of prophetic critiques of the leaders of Israel, when such leaders lost perspective about the priorities of the law. The Torah is "not a uniform codex"; there are weightier commands that have priority, above all those enjoining love and compassion for the neighbor (22:40). These laws have priority over the cultic laws, as the controversy stories in Matthew illustrate (see, for example, 12:1–8, 9–14).

Throughout his book Sand emphasizes that the ultimate purpose of Matthew's discussions about the law was not to counteract the Pharisees (although this was an obvious influence). The scribes and the Pharisees and other opponents stand as a generalized portrait, similar to the opponents of the classical prophets, those whose interpretation of law and fidelity to that law was lacking. Matthew's primary goal was *paranesis* or exhortation to the Christian community itself. His concern was theological and pastoral: to emphasize the necessity of "doing God's will." Such was the intent of the Torah itself, and the preaching of Jesus had the same goal. Such obedience is to be gauged by its "fruit" (see 7:13–14, 15–20; 12:34). Those who fail to do God's will, substituting mere words for action, are liable to judgment (21:18–19, 33–46).

Another goal of Sand's book is to study the significance of the phrase "the law and the prophets" (Mt. 5:17; 22:40) as indicative of Matthew's theological perspective. He notes that in the Old Testament there was already an intrinsic connection between the functions of the Torah and the ministry of the prophets: both, albeit in different ways, had as their goal the revelation of God's salvific will to Israel, particularly his care for the weak and defenseless. Jesus' own proclamation of the kingdom of God definitively affirmed and newly interpreted what had always been the message of the "law and the prophets." Thus this phrase should not be taken as two divisions of the biblical literature but as a summary of God's will for Israel, now brought to positive fulfillment in Jesus' ministry to the outcasts and his proclamation of the love command. Jesus' emphasis on the love command as the supreme norm of the law and the prophets ultimately defines what is meant by "righteousness" (3:15; 5:20) in Matthew.[11]

Sand's excellent study not only deals effectively with many of the complexities of Matthew's attitude to the law, but also correctly links this issue, not to theological speculation or merely to polemic attacks on the community's opponents, but to the pastoral, exhortational concerns of Matthew.

John Meier in his book *Law and History in Matthew's Gospel* (1976) and in a more popular version of that study, *The Vision of Matthew* (1979), also attempts to fit Matthew's attitude to the law into the totality of the Gospel.[12] If we give Meier's work a brief treatment here, it is not because his contribution is unimportant but simply because we have already laid out his major thesis in our discussion of salvation history.

As we pointed out in that earlier discussion, Meier fits the law issue into Matthew's theology of history. Rigorist statements about the law's perduring validity (5:18) can be reconciled with *de facto* abrogations of the law (for example, on divorce, oaths, talion; cf. 5:30–42) because the death and resurrection of Jesus is a radical turning point in sacred history. The law was fully enforced "until heaven and earth pass away," "until all is accomplished" (5:18)—but the old age has effectively passed away and a new one has begun in the apocalyptic events of Jesus's death and resurrection.

Similar to Banks and Sand, Meier sees the meaning of the word "fulfill" best understood in terms of prophetic fulfillment. The Hebrew Scriptures find their ultimate meaning in the risen Christ; they pointed toward Jesus and find their destiny in him. Matthew, Meier concludes, did not envision Jesus' mission as the dissolution of the law and the prophets. "His mission has rather the positive scope of giving the law and the prophets their eschatological fulfillment, a prophetic fullness which rescinds the letter of the law even as it completes its meaning. Jesus is the Messiah who brings consummation, not the revolutionary who brings desolation."[13]

Conclusion

The law question has taken us deeply into Matthew's theology. While many points are still debated, there are important points of convergence: (1) The law issue is not simply a matter of Matthew's struggle against outside opponents (for example, the synagogue) but goes to the heart of his message to his church. (2) The law issue is closely linked to Christology: Jesus' authority as the risen Christ underwrites the Church's interpretation of law. (3) Apparent contradictions among some of Matthew's law texts might best be explained by taking into account different layers of tradition within the Gospel.

6
Matthew's Christology

Introduction

Every aspect of Matthew's theology is ultimately connected with his convictions about the identity and meaning of Jesus. This should be evident from the topics we have already considered: Matthew's schema of salvation history, no matter how interpreters outline it, pivots around the Jesus event; Matthew's interpretation of the Old Testament Scriptures is controlled by his conviction about Jesus' identity as the Messiah; again, no matter how one interprets the fine points, it remains true that the role of law in Matthew's perspective is essentially linked to the authority of the risen Christ; "righteousness" is now defined as fidelity to the teaching of Jesus.

Our goal in this chapter is not to attempt a comprehensive treatment of Christology in Matthew—a step that might have us tread ground we have already covered—but to sample recent scholarship on select issues in Matthew's portrayal of Jesus. Three topics have gained considerable attention in recent exegesis: (1) the role of Christological titles in Matthew; (2) the use of Wisdom motifs; (3) Matthew's emphasis on Jesus as healer.

Titles Applied to Jesus

Any student of the New Testament is aware that titles such as Son of God, Christ, Lord, etc., were important expressions of early Christological reflection.[1]

One of the most comprehensive studies of Matthew's use of titles for Jesus has been the work of Jack Dean Kingsbury, *Matthew: Structure, Christology, Kingdom.*[2] Kingsbury examines each of the major titles in Matthew and attempts to establish some hierarchy and interrelationship among them.

The pre-eminent title in Matthew's Christology, Kingsbury claims, is "Son of God." This is the one title that occurs in every major section of the Gospel and correlates with essential features of Matthew's overall theology. In the opening section of the narrative, 1:1—4:16, the first explicit designation of Jesus as "Son" is at the baptism in 3:17, but Matthew has prepared for this in the infancy narratives of chapters 1–2. The virginal conception insures that Jesus' origin is from God (1:18–20); he is "Emmanuel," "God-with-us" (1:23) and "savior" (1:21)—all indications of his status as Son of God. Kingsbury believes that the references to "the child" and "the child and his mother" (2:11, 13–14, 20–21) also allude to Jesus' divine sonship. The title is not explicitly applied to Jesus until 3:17 (although see 2:15 where "my son" is used in the quote from Hosea 11:1) because Jesus' identity as Son of God is a *revelation* from the Father, a revelation that points to the deepest mystery of Jesus' existence.

The title's presence continues in key moments throughout the Gospel. Kingsbury admits that in the long section 4:17 to 10:42 it occurs only once (8:29); the main reason for this, he believes, is that the Son of God title is a *confessional* title, not to be used in a "public" or non-confessional way. The demon's use of the title in 8:29 is a valid exception because supernatural beings understand who Jesus is. However, even in this section, Kingsbury finds hints of the Son of God designation for Jesus. He teaches on the *mountain* (5:1), a place of revelation, of communication with the divine, and of authority. In chapters 5–7 Jesus is depicted as authoritative teacher, in 8–9 as powerful healer. The disciples Jesus chooses and empowers for mission are designated "sons of God" (5:9) or "sons of your heavenly Father" (5:45). All of these texts show that Jesus' identity as Son of God is a capital point for Matthew even when the title is not cited.

In subsequent sections of the Gospel, important and explicit "Son of God" texts emerge. In 11:25–27 Jesus designates himself as Son. The disciples dramatically confess Jesus as Son of God after he appears to them walking on the waters of the lake (14:33). Peter does the same at Caesarea Philippi (16:13–20). In the transfiguration story, the confessional and revelational aspects of the title are again evident as the voice from heaven declares Jesus as "my beloved son" (17:1–8). The saying of Jesus about being "in the midst" of the disciples (18:20) recalls the Emmanuel text of 1:23. The parable of the wicked tenants (21:33–46) who kill the son sent as messenger and the parable of the great supper a king gives for his son (22:1–10) again pick up the motif. The title also plays a significant role in the passion story: Jesus prays "my Father" in Gethsemene (26:39, 42); the charge of the high priest centers around Jesus' identity as "Son of God" (26:63). The title is especially prominent at the climactic death scene: the mockers challenge Jesus' identity as "Son of God" (27:40, 43), and in response to Jesus' death and the marvelous signs that accompany it (27:51–53), the centurion and his companions solemnly confess: "Truly this was the Son of God" (27:54).

Even though there is no explicit use of the title in the concluding scene of the Gospel (28:16–20) Kingsbury believes that a Son of God Christology is operative there, too. The reference to Jesus' authority in 28:18 refers to his identity as the risen Son of God, an authority challenged in mockery at the crucifixion but now vindicated through resurrection. Kingsbury finds many connections between this final commission scene and other key passages in which the Son of God title had appeared. It is on a mountain (compare 17:1–8), and there is a reference to the doubt of the disciples (compare 14:31–33), a reference to baptism (compare 3:16–17), and the promise of abiding presence (as in 1:23).

Therefore, Matthew portrays Jesus as Son of God from start to finish. It is a title that touches all aspects of Jesus' ministry and confirms his divine authority.

Although Kingsbury focuses on the Son of God title he does not ignore other important titles in Matthew. "Son of David" is one of Matthew's favorites (he applies it to Jesus ten times, compared with four each in Mark and Luke).[3] This title stresses Jesus' role as the Davidic Messiah sent to Israel and also serves to focus on the guilt of Israel for not accepting him. Matthew signals this by having Jesus perform healing acts for outcasts such as the blind, the lame, and the Gentiles. These insignificant people acclaim Jesus as "Son of David" (cf. 21:5; 15:21-22) while Israelites reject him. But ultimately the Son of David title is subordinate to and redefined by Jesus' identity as Son of God. This latter title also has messianic meaning in Israel but in Matthew's Gospel its connotation goes beyond mere messianic identity for Jesus.

"Son of Man" is also an important title in Matthew, as it is in Mark. But Kingsbury feels it is subordinate to the Son of God title. The Son of Man title is "public" in character, that is, "it serves to describe Jesus in terms of his relationship to the world, Israel first and then the Gentiles, and especially as he interacts with the crowds and his opponents" (p. 121). As already illustrated, Kingsbury sees the Son of God title, by contrast, as a confessional title in Matthew, conveying what for the believing Church is the "deepest mystery concerning the person of Jesus: his origin is in God and therefore it is in him that God dwells with his people. . . . As the Son of God, Jesus presides over and resides in his Church until the end of the age, at which time he will confront both Church and world as, again, the Son of Man" (pp. 121-22).

Kingsbury studies all of the major titles in Matthew, but we will report his comments on only one other, that of "Lord" (*Kyrios*). Many scholars contend that this is Matthew's most significant title,[4] but Kingsbury disagrees. He concedes that it is an important title in the Gospel attributing "an exalted station to Jesus and one that is specifically divine" (p. 106), as in 12:8 where Jesus is declared "Lord of the sabbath." But the title cannot claim first rank because in almost all instances "Lord" refers to the authority Jesus bears precisely on the basis of some further designation such as "Son of Man," "Son of David," or "Son of God." For example in 24:42 the community is warned that in the final days "your Lord is coming." But this authority as "Lord" derives from Jesus' designation as the Son of Man who will come in judgment (cf. 24:37, 39, 44). The same kind of relationship exists with the Son of God title: in 14:28 and 30 Peter appeals to Jesus for power to walk on the water and to be saved when he begins to sink, but this authority of Jesus is based on his identity as Son of God as the confession at the end of the scene reveals (14:33). Therefore, Kingsbury concludes, the "Lord" title is "derivative," pointing beyond itself to more definitive Christological terms.

Kingsbury's treatment of titles in Matthew is thorough and coherent but has had a mixed reception among scholars. Some feel that he presses too hard for a comprehensive pattern in Matthew's use of titles for Jesus. Many would agree that "Son of God" is a key title and Kingsbury deserves credit for stressing its importance. But over-emphasis on this title may devalue other theological categories in Matthew. Dennis Hill in a recent article entitled "Son and Servant: An Essay on Matthean Christology" criticizes Kingsbury on this very point.[5] He contends that in some major sections of the Gospel the image of "Servant of Yahweh" shapes Matthew's concept of Jesus as Son of God. Servant typology was important to Matthew as the long quote from Isaiah 42:1–4 in 12:17–21 demonstrates.[6] The qualities of meekness and compassion exemplified by the servant are essential qualities of Jesus' own messiahship.[7]

Other scholars have questioned whether the relationship between Son of God and Son of Man titles in Matthew is that of confessional versus public, with the Son of Man in a subordinate position. The strongest challenge on this score comes from John Meier who directly dialogues with Kingsbury's position in his book, *The Vision of Matthew*.[8] First of all, Meier is convinced that it is a Son of Man, not Son of God Christology which influences the final scene of the Gospel (28:16–20). An important clue is 28:18 ("all authority on heaven and earth has been given to me"); this text appears to be an allusion to Daniel 7:13, a passage that refers to the future coming of a mysterious "Son of Man" (see also Mt. 26:64 where the Daniel text is cited). The triumphant meeting between the risen Jesus and his disciples in 28:16–20 is, in Meier's phrase, a "proleptic parousia," an anticipation of the final coming of the Son of Man in triumph and judgment at the end of the world (cf. Mt. 24:30). The Son of Man has, in one sense, already come to his community to empower them for mission and to be with them until the end of time.

Meier further contends that Son of Man Christology plays a positive role in the rest of Matthew's Gospel; it is not reserved to merely public, non-confessional contexts or reserved only for future judgment. The title occurs some thirty times (Son of God occurs only nine times plus three times as "my Son" uttered by God), in contexts that span the full range of Gospel events: Jesus' servanthood (20:28), his authority to forgive sins (9:6), as friend of sinners (11:19), as "Lord of the sabbath" (12:8), as suffering, dying and rising Servant (17:12, 22; 20:18, 26:2), as final judge coming in glory (10:23; 13:41; 16:27–28; 19:28; 24:27, 30, 37, 39, 44; 25:31). It is a title with a significance of its own for Matthew and should not be "swallowed up" by the "Son of God" title.

Meier makes a further suggestion: we should not think of any title as *the* central one. *Both* Son of God and Son of Man titles are important to Matthew. Perhaps when the Gospel refers to Jesus simply as "the Son," the evangelist had in mind Jesus' dual identity as Son of God (with its messianic and transcendent dimension) and Son of Man (with its emphasis on suffering, compassion, and final victorious judgment). In this issue, as in some others we have considered, Gospel interpretation is best served when the interpreter does not demand too much systematization from the Gospel writer.

Jesus as Wisdom of God

One aspect of Matthew's christology just beginning to come under scrutiny is his use of Wisdom motifs. A pioneer in this area is M. Jack Suggs in his book, *Wisdom, Christology and Law in Matthew's Gospel.*[9]

The lynchpin of Suggs' position is the hypothesis that Matthew used Q as a source. That early Christian document, Suggs contends, was itself influenced by Jewish and early Christian speculation on "Wisdom," the revelation of God to Israel as metaphorically reflected on in the so-called Wisdom literature of Israel (see such books as the Wisdom of Solomon, Proverbs, Sirach, etc.).[10] The Q document may have drawn on a now lost Jewish "wisdom apocalypse," a series of oracles describing Wisdom's mission of revealing God to Israel, the sending of her emissaries in pursuit of this mission, and Wisdom's withdrawal from Israel in judgment on their rejection (Suggs finds traces of such a Wisdom myth in Proverbs 1:20, 21, 24–31). In Q Jesus himself would be presented as one of Wisdom's rejected messengers; thus Q did not develop a genuine Christology as such but presented Jesus only in the light of Jewish Wisdom speculation.

Matthew, on the other hand, reinterprets Q, significantly escalating its portrayal of Jesus. Suggs focuses on only a few key texts. In 23:34–36, for example, *Jesus himself* is presented as "prophet and wise man and scribe" to Israel. The Q text which Matthew used as a source would have spoken of *Wisdom* sending Jesus; Matthew makes *Jesus* himself personified Wisdom, the revealer of God. A similar interpretation is detected in 11:2–19. The passage reviews the "deeds of the Christ" (11:2) and concludes with the saying, "Wisdom is justified by her deeds" (11:19). The parallel passage in Luke 7:35 speaks of Wisdom justified "by all *her children.*" Luke's version reflects the original wording of Q which identified John the Baptist and Jesus as emissaries (i.e., "children") of Wisdom. But Matthew's changes identify *Jesus* as personified Wisdom whose deeds reveal God. In the latter part of chapter 11 Suggs finds further influences of Wisdom Christology. Matthew 11:25–30 draws on a Wisdom hymn which is now applied no longer to the Torah as revealer of God (as in the Book of Sirach) but to Jesus who is in communion with the Father and makes him known, and whose yoke is easy and light.

In these texts, Suggs claims, we have significant evidence that Matthew used Wisdom speculation to present Jesus as the personified Wisdom of God, a crucial step in the development of New Testament Christology.[11]

Some have been reluctant to accept Suggs' view. Marshall Johnson in an article entitled "Reflections on a Wisdom Approach to Matthew's Christology"[12] questions Suggs' hypothesis about a lost "Wisdom apocalypse" behind the Q document and wonders if Wisdom speculation had developed such a full-blown myth about Wisdom's emissaries. And what evidence do we really have that Matthew intensified Wisdom speculation in regard to Christ, since we cannot be sure of his sources?

Suggs' hypothesis about a lost Wisdom apocalypse is the weakest part of his argument, but other exegetes have supported his contention that, in any case, Wisdom motifs play a significant role in Matthew's Christology. A recent book by Fred W. Burnett, *The Testament of Jesus-Sophia,* presses on with some of the issues raised but not addressed by Suggs' groundbreaking study.[13] Burnett maintains that the entire eschatological discourse of Matthew 24:3–31 can be seen under the guise of Jesus as Wisdom. The discourse is Jesus/ Wisdom's final testament to his disciples (= Wisdom's emissaries) after this rejection by Israel (cf. ch. 23).

In Johannine studies it is generally agreed that Wisdom motifs were instrumental in enabling the evangelist to make a conceptual breakthrough in expressing his convictions about Jesus as pre-existent and incarnate Word of God.[14] One can be sure that further work will be done on the influence of Wisdom metaphors in Matthew's Christology as well.

Jesus as Healer

The dominant presence of the Sermon on the Mount in Matthew 5—7 and the other great discourses of the Gospel, plus the Gospel's concern with Jesus as interpreter of Law, leaves little doubt that Matthew presents Jesus as the definitive *teacher*. In fact, the disciples are reminded that there is only "one Teacher" and one "Master," Jesus himself (23:8, 10).

Less obvious, perhaps, is the fact that Matthew also lays great emphasis on Jesus' role as healer. A ground-breaking and still important analysis of this dimension of Matthew's Christology is that of Heinz Joachim Held, "Matthew as Interpreter of the Miracle Stories," first appearing as a doctoral dissertation in 1957.[15] Held focused mainly on the collection of miracle stories in chapters 8–9, a section of the Gospel long recognized as a significant unit. Held's extensive analysis not only yielded rich results for understanding Matthew's theology but was a model of redaction criticism.

Held affirmed what previous scholars had already noted: that in this section of the Gospel Matthew groups and re-edits a string of miracle stories found in his source Mark (with the exception of the cure of the centurion's servant which was drawn from Q; cf. Mt. 8:5–13; Lk. 7:1–10 and several sayings). Matthew has framed the entire unit of the Sermon on the Mount (chs. 5—7) and the miracles (chs. 8—9) with two identical summaries (4:23 and 9:35) which stress Jesus' *teaching* and *healing,* activities illustrated in the intervening chapters.

Matthew's re-editing and reinterpretation of Mark's material are extensive. He radically abbreviates Mark's stories (compare Mt. 8:28–34 with Mk. 5:1–20), not haphazardly, but in order to expand or highlight discourse material. The end result is a threefold grouping of the ten miracles into three major sections, each of which stresses a particular theme: Christology in 8:1–17 (the power of Jesus to heal), discipleship in 8:18–9:17 (the necessity of following Jesus wherever he goes), and faith in 9:1–17 (Jesus' response to the "praying faith" of his community).

Although subsequent studies have gone beyond Held's work, all use it as point of departure.[16] Two examples of alternate approaches will have to suffice. As part of his continuing investigation of Matthew's Christology, J. D. Kingsbury has also analyzed chapters 8–9.[17] While accepting Held's basic conclusions, Kingsbury adds some qualifications. First of all, following the lead of Christoph Burger,[18] he prefers to see a *four*fold thematic division of the entire section: (1) 8:1–17 on Christology; (2) 8:18–34 on discipleship; (3) 9:1–17 on the separation of Jesus and his followers from Israel (this subsection is a refinement of Held's original three-part division); (4) 9:18–34 on faith.

In line with his thesis discussed earlier, Kingsbury maintains that the entire miracle section presents Jesus primarily as the powerful Son of God. Even though this title is not explicitly used, the Son of God Christology, already proclaimed in the opening chapters (1–4), carries over. Kingsbury concedes that Matthew cites the Servant text of Isaiah 53:4 in connection with the healing activity of Jesus (Mt. 8:17; see also Mt. 12:17–21, a quote of Is. 42:1–4, which is again applied to Jesus' healing activity), but in such key texts as 3:17 and 17:5 Matthew combines quotes from the Servant Songs of Isaiah 42:1–4 with Psalm 2:7 which designates Jesus as *Son.* Therefore, he argues, the Servant title is subordinate to Matthew's Son of God Christology.

Kingsbury also stresses the significance of the miracle stories for Matthew's theology of discipleship. The Gospel presents Jesus as the powerful Son of God in the midst of Israel (8:1, 10, 18; 9:8, 33), healing his people and gathering disciples (8:18–22; 9:9). These chapters are meant to be a lesson for Matthew's church, setting forth "the cost and commitment of discipleship and ways in which they are distinct from contemporary Israel (8:18–22, 23–27; 9:1–17)" (pp. 572–573). Matthew's Christians are invited to approach the exalted Son of God present within the community and to express their need, confident of his divine power.

The Scandanavian scholar Birger Gerhardsson has also examined the miracle stories in his book, *The Mighty Acts of Jesus According to Matthew.*[19] Gerhardsson covers the full range of miracles in the

Gospel, not only the collection in chapters 8–9, but other stories and summaries of Jesus' deeds throughout the Gospel. He makes a distinction between "therapeutic" stories such as the healings which are generally on the demand of the sick person, are scattered throughout Jesus' ministry, and are directed to the people or individual "outsiders," and "non-therapeutic" miracles (an example would be the stilling of the storm or the walking on the water), which, by contrast, are more occasional, are not mentioned in the summaries, are done at Jesus' invitation, and are performed exclusively for disciples. Gerhardsson concludes from this that the "non-therapeutic" miracle stories have a more problematic historical basis and are probably to be located more within the Christological reflection of the early Church.

Gerhardsson stresses the importance of the stories and references to Jesus' miracles for Matthew's Christology. The Gospel uses this material to portray Jesus' "incomparable *exousia* (= power) as *the healer of Israel*" (p. 93). Rather than a Christology subsumed under and dominated by the Son of God designation (as Kingsbury insists), Gerhardsson believes that Matthew's Christology was "many-faceted," a portrayal of Jesus "illustrated with many kinds of material" (p. 82). Many titles appear in connection with the mighty acts of Jesus: "Son of Man," "Christ," "Son of David," "Lord," etc. He agrees with Kingsbury that "Son of God" is Matthew's most important designation for Jesus. However, the title of Jesus as Servant is not submerged by the Son title but, in fact, qualifies Jesus' role as Son of God. He is Son of God precisely in that he is humble, obedient and serving. The Son of God title is not applied to Jesus in the healing stories whereas Servant texts are (see Mt. 8:17; 12:18). Thus the therapeutic activity brings out a dimension of Matthew's Christology which the exalted title "Son of God" does not. In fact none of the titles is essential to the miracle stories; the *narratives themselves* present Christology by showing Jesus in action.

Conclusion

Our survey of what scholars are saying about Matthew's Christology gives some idea of the Gospel's extraordinary richness. Frustration in finding *the* dominant category demonstrates Gerhardsson's sage observation about the multifaceted perspective of Matthew. The Jesus reverenced by his church could not be contained even by categories as forceful as Teacher, Healer, Son of God, Son of Man, Lord, Wisdom incarnate or triumphant Son of Man. The object of Matthew's reflection rendered all categories inadequate. That perhaps is one of the reasons the evangelist portrays Jesus by means of a story, a narrative in which Old Testament reflection, Christological titles, and vignettes of Jesus in action are all blended to convey his experience of Jesus' presence within the community.

7
The Church in Matthew's Gospel

Introduction

Similar to the preceding chapter on Christology, a study of Matthew's view of the Church takes us into almost every area of the Gospel. There is, of course, no systematic or formal description of Church life in the Gospel, no theological treatise on ecclesiology. Matthew's vision of the Church must be deduced from the character of his story about Jesus, the disciples, and the other events and players in the Gospel drama. Matthew's story is a story from the past but its intent is contemporary to the life of the evangelist and his community. This ecclesial interest of Matthew is evident from features of the Gospel such as the discourse on community life in chapter 18, not to mention the fact he uses the technical term *ekklesia* or "Church" three times (16:18; 18:17), the only evangelist to do so.

What contemporary scholars have to say about Church in Matthew has, in part, already been described in the preceding chapters. The discussion on the milieu of the Gospel (chapter 1) gives some idea about the probable atmosphere and make-up of Matthew's community: an urban, prosperous, Greek-speaking church composed of Jews and Gentiles, caught up in the tension of a critical transition moment. The chapter on salvation history dealt with how Matthew situated the existence of the Church in relation to the phenomenon of Israel. The chapter on Matthew's use of the Old Testament added further profile to Matthew's church: in the view of some scholars, a Greek-speaking church well versed in the art of biblical interpretation, a church that saw Jesus (and, therefore, the community founded in his name) as the fulfillment of the promises made to Israel. The chapter on law added further insight. Matthew's church was enough in tune with Judaism to stress continuity with the "law and the prophets" but found, in the teaching of Jesus, its authority and norm for radically reinterpreting the law. The Torah of Jesus as presented by Matthew's Gospel stressed the need for "righteousness," obedience to God's will expressed in good deeds, especially acts of compassion toward the neighbor. Here some of Matthew's special portrayal of the disciples finds its basis. And, finally, the chapter on Christology discussed Matthew's portrayal of Jesus as the basis for all Christian existence and, therefore, as the foundation for ecclesiology.

Therefore, issues of Matthew's ecclesiology can be found in almost every aspect of the Gospel. Our goal in this chapter will be to consider a few remaining elements not yet explicitly dealt with.

A Theological Basis for Church

An important study of Matthew's vision of church is that of Hubert Frankemölle, *Jahwebund and Kirche Christ.*[1] Because he attempts a synthesis of Matthew's ecclesiology it may be worthwhile to begin our discussion with a summary of his thesis.

Frankemölle locates the keystone of Matthew's theology of church in the bond between the community and the risen Christ, a point few would contest. Matthew's model for this, Frankemölle contends, is the Old Testament covenant between Yahweh and Israel, especially as that covenant theology was interpreted by the Deuteronomist and Chronicler. Matthew's recurring phrase "with us" or "with you" is, in effect, a covenant formula expressing Jesus' bond with the community. In 1:23, for example, Jesus' very name is Emmanuel, God-with-us." In 17:17 Jesus laments, "How long am I to be with you?" In 18:20 the formula occurs again, expressing the risen Christ's solidarity with two or three of his disciples gathered in prayer. Matthew's presentation of the Last Supper (26:29) and Jesus' prayer in Gethsemene (26:38, 40) adds the key phrases "with you" and "with me"—both expressing the deep covenant bond. The concluding scene of 28:16–20 reaffirms the continuing presence of the risen Christ in his Church. This latter text, by the way, Frankemölle sees as modeled on the conclusion of the Second Book of Chronicles (26:23).[2]

In these and similar texts of Matthew's Gospel, Jesus is presented as bound to his community just as Yahweh was bound to Israel. This "covenant" is the source and norm for the community's existence. The reality of this new covenant answers the theological problem of God's fidelity to Israel. Even though Israel rejected the Gospel, God is faithful in that he forms a new covenant through Jesus.

Frankemölle sees this covenant theology borne out in other elements of Matthew's portrayal of the Church, especially his portrayal of the disciples and their mission. Through their bond with Jesus, the disciples are designated "sons" of God. (See for example, 5:9, 45; 8:12; 13:38; 17:25–26; 23:9). This, in turn, establishes a deep bond among the disciples/church members. They are the family of Jesus (12:46–50) and their relationship as brother and sister must be expressed in mutual respect and compassion (18:15–35).

Besides such "individual-personal" concepts as disciple, Frankemölle also examines collective symbols such as "people" (*laos*) and "church" (*ekklesia*). In each case these are drawn from Old Testament sources (especially Deuteronomy) but take on new meaning in the light of Matthew's covenant ecclesiology. In Deuteronomy the term "people" referred to those made such by God's gracious covenant; God would remain faithful but the "people" were capable of rejecting God and disobeying the covenant. In 1:21 and 27:24–25 Frankemölle sees this polarity of meaning present in a new context. In 1:21 "people" refers to all, Jews and Gentiles, who will be offered God's gracious salvation through Jesus. But in 27:24–25 Matthew indicates that those who reject Jesus thereby lose their status as God's people. Matthew attempts to fit Israel's rejection of the Gospel into a long-standing biblical tradition.

The term *ekklesia* or "Church," according to Frankemölle, is also steeped in covenant theology. Matthew's designation "my (that is, Jesus') Church" (16:18) draws its inspiration from Deuteronomy and Chronicles which speak of Israel as "Yahweh's *ekklesia*" or assembly: the "Church" is the faithful remnant who through fidelity to the covenant truly belongs to God's people. For Matthew, too, the "Church" or assembly of God's people means those who accept Jesus as a new expression of the covenant.

Frankemölle relates almost every aspect of Matthew's Gospel to this basic covenant model. The demand for obedience to the will of the Father, the law as newly interpreted and grounded by Christ, the mission to the Gentiles (a people capable of belonging to God's people through faith in Jesus), judgment on Israel and those who fail in this covenant obligation—all these aspects of Christian existence find their ultimate synthesis in Matthew's concept of the Church as the new covenant community.

Not all would accept Frankemölle's singular emphasis on covenant as the major motif of Matthew's ecclesiology. If in fact the Church so definitively replaced Israel, it would seem logical for Matthew to name the Church the "new Israel."[3] But in fact Matthew does not go that far. While the covenant motif may be less dominant than Frankemölle suggests, many of the aspects of Matthew's ecclesiology he stresses are valid. Surely Matthew does highlight the personal bond between Jesus and the community, and he does see Jesus' mission as the fulfillment of the Old Testament promises. Likewise Matthew does present Israel's rejection of Jesus as a failure with historic consequences resulting in the inclusion of Gentiles (see, for example, 21:43). And, finally, belonging to Jesus' Church does involve faith in Christ and obedience to the will of the Father as taught by Jesus. It is in these elements of discipleship that further insight into Matthew's ecclesiology can be gained.

Discipleship in Matthew

A number of scholars have offered detailed studies of discipleship in Matthew, and there seems to be considerable consensus about the broad features of this part of the Gospel.[4]

A recent work which attempts a more comprehensive synthesis of the issue is Jean Zumstein's *La Condition du Croyant dans L'Évangile selon Matthieu* ("The Situation of the Believer in the Gospel According to Matthew").[5] His treatment can help us review the essential data.

Zumstein's basic thesis is that through his portrayal of the disciples Matthew describes the qualities of Christian existence—a point few scholars would dispute. Matthew presents the disciples as a homogenous and specific group, distinct from both "the crowds," who form a neutral group and are the object of Jesus' ministry,[6] and Jesus' various opponents who symbolize those who reject Jesus.[7] The disciples are the privileged companions of Jesus and are defended by him. Similar to Frankemölle and others, Zumstein finds the theological foundation for Matthew's identification of "disciples" with Christians in the on-going bond of the risen Christ with his Church. Texts such as 28:16–20, 5:17–20, and 11:25–30 affirm the continuing presence and authority of Christ in the community.

By closely examining various categories in the Gospel, Zumstein believes we can add further coloration to a portrayal of the Matthean church. For example, favorable references to "scribes" suggest that they had a leadership role in Matthew's church as interpreters of tradition (13:52) and as ones responsible for mission work, perhaps among their Jewish brethren (23:34). Prophets also played a role in the Church, but a diminishing one after the catastrophe of A.D. 70 because one of their main responsibilities was mission work among the Jews (see 5:12; 10:41; 23:34, 37). At several points in the Gospel there are hints of problems and tensions: "lawlessness" (7:23; 24:12), "scandal" (18:5–9), "divisions" (10:21), persecutions (10:17–15), etc. The Church is a mixture of good and bad, of wheat and tares until the end of time (13:24–30, 36–43, 47–50).

Most of Zumstein's efforts are concentrated on the disciples as presented by Matthew. The Matthean disciples "understand" Jesus. This is a sharp contrast from Mark where the disciples often fail to comprehend Jesus (compare Mk. 6:52 and Mt. 14:33; Mk 8:19 and Mt. 16:12). Matthew does not idealize the disciples; they are still capable of failure, but, much more evidently than in Mark, the disciples are able to penetrate the mystery of Jesus' identity. Such sympathetic comprehension of Jesus and his teaching is a quality of Christian existence (13:23, 51). The disciple is also expected to hear the call of Christ (4:18–22; 9:9) and to "follow" him (8:18–22), leaving behind his or her former mode of existence (10:37–39). The disciples, of course, must have "faith" in Christ, putting complete trust in him, especially in the midst of trial and crisis, a point frequently illustrated in the miracle stories (see, for example, 8:10, 13; 9:2, 22, 28–29, etc.). The disciple must also extend such confident faith to the future, waiting in active vigilance for the unexpected coming of the Master (24:27–44,15–51; 25:1–13).

A special emphasis of Matthew is the theme of "little faith," a term the evangelist discovers in Q (see Mt. 6:3; Lk. 12:28) but further develops (8:26; 14:31; 16:8; 17:20). The Gospel recognizes that the world is a dangerous place which can provoke a crisis of faith, leading to the paralysis of "doubt" (14:31; 28:17) and fear (14:30) even as one believes.

As was noted in our chapter on the law, the Gospel is concerned with what Zumstein calls the "ethical" response of the disciple/ believer. The starting point of all ethical response, according to Zumsteim, is the "gracious offer of eschatological happiness" (see, for example, the Beatitudes of 5:2–12); the challenge for discipleship is "by what decision of life do I respond" to this gracious offer? Guidance for that response is found throughout the Gospel in such texts as the radical teaching of the Sermon on the Mount with its call for "love of enemies" and being "perfect as your heavenly Father is perfect" (5:43–48), and in the judgment parables such as 25:31–46.

The "Church" according to Matthew is, therefore, the assembly of those who respond in faith and obedience to the invitation of the coming kingdom (22:1–14; 21:33–46). The Church is not to be identified with the kingdom; there are various levels of response as one moves toward the final consummation of history (13:36–43, 47–50). True greatness within the Church is to be marked by concern for the weak members (18:6–14), by "fraternal discipline" (18:15–20) and limitless forgiveness (18:21–35).[8] At the same time, the community is to give to the world the witness of good deeds (5:13–16) and is to be involved in active proclamation of the Gospel of the kingdom (10:1, 7–8) to all nations (28:16–20).

Zumstein's discussion of discipleship does not break much new ground but effectively synthesizes many of the results of Matthean scholarship. One lacuna in his study, however, is the role of Peter in

Matthew's Gospel, an important aspect of the Gospel that will conclude our study.

Peter: Representative Disciple or Symbol of Leadership?

A baffling element of Matthew's view of discipleship and Church is the role of Peter. A comparison of Matthew with his probable source Mark reveals that our evangelist has significantly inflated the role of Peter. Matthew retains such important Markan texts where Peter is the first one called (4:18) and the one who confesses Jesus (16:16) but adds several unique Petrine passages such as Peter's walking on the water (14:28–31), Jesus' special blessing of Peter (16:17–19), the story of the temple tax (17:24–27) and the discussion about forgiveness (18:21–22). While greater prominence is given to Peter, the evangelist does not gloss over negative traditions about Peter such as his attempt to dissuade Jesus from the cross (16:22–23) or Peter's denial (26:33–35, 69–75). In some instances Matthew portrays Peter in a worse light than Mark does (see, for example, the addition of the word "scandal" in 16:23).

So the figure of Peter in Matthew's Gospel is a "mixed" portrayal: a prominent spokesman for the disciples, blessed by Jesus, yet also fearful, weak in faith, an obstacle to Jesus, and capable of outright failure.

Biblical scholarship has been divided over how to interpret Peter's role in the Gospel. Two main trends can be detected in recent studies. (1) Some see Peter's role as merely "representative," that is, Peter dramatizes the positive and the negative qualities of all Christian disciples. He does not represent anything beyond that, such as a type or symbol of leadership within the community. (2) Other scholars move in a different direction: they concede that Peter does serve as a "representative disciple" but believe that the strong focus on Peter indicates something more.

This issue, of course, has important ecumenical implications since Roman Catholicism has traditionally appealed to Petrine texts such as Matthew 16:16–19 as a biblical foundation for the papal office. Happily most exegetical studies of Matthew's Gospel have moved beyond mere apologetics for later Church positions, Catholic or Protestant. Few Roman Catholic scholars, for example, would construe Jesus' words to Peter in Mt. 16:16–19 as the installation of the first Pope. And most Protestant scholars survey the biblical evidence on Peter without the object of discrediting the papacy. At the same time, however, the role of Peter in Matthew and in other New Testament texts may be important evidence for emerging structures in the early Church, so contemporary ecumenical discussion cannot be divorced from exegesis of these passages.

Two Matthean scholars, one Lutheran and one Roman Catholic, each of them dealing with the data in a competent and objective fashion can help us see the state of the art on this issue.

In his article "The Figure of Peter in Matthew's Gospel as a Theological Problem," Jack Dean Kingsbury holds the position that Peter, while an important figure in Matthew's Gospel, is, nevertheless, a representative figure "squarely within the circle of the disciples."[9] Kingsbury sifts through all the data, noting the attention Matthew gives to Peter but finding that in each instance the evangelist ascribes to the other disciples the same functions given to Peter such as "binding and loosing" (16:19 and 18:18), being declared "blessed" (16:17 and 13:16–17), confessing Jesus as "Son of God" (16:16 and 14:33), and so on.[10]

Kingsbury concedes one point to those who believe Peter has a special position: Peter enjoys a "salvation-historical primacy." Peter and the rest of the Gospel cast are figures "from the past" as well as types for discipleship within the present of Matthew's church. In this salvation-history perspective, Peter plays a primary role as the first called (4:18) and as spokesman for the disciples. It is this "historical" role that Matthew expands in his story, in comparison with Mark. But this type of primacy does not put Peter outside the circle of the disciples; he is merely *primus inter pares.* The Church in Matthew is egalitarian in nature: while some exercise different functions such as teacher (13:52; 23:8–10) there are no "offices." No one has rank over another (23:8–13); the entire community holds authority (18:18–20). Jesus as the exalted Messiah and Son of God is the one who guides and rules the Church (18:18–20; 23:8–10; 28:18–20).

Looking at the same evidence, other scholars have reached different conclusions. A significant study is the book *Peter in the New Testament,* an examination of all the New Testament material on Peter by an ecumenical team of scholars.[11] Raymond Brown, who was a Roman Catholic participant in the study, synthesizes some of its results in an essay entitled "The Meaning of Modern New Testament Studies for an Ecumenical Understanding of Peter and a Theology of the Papacy."[12] The treatment of Matthew in these two works can illustrate the trend running counter to Kingsbury's position.

Both positions agree in many points and share a common methodology. Brown, for example, agrees that in most passages of Matthew Peter acts as a representative figure, exemplifying positive and negative features of Christian discipleship. And he would also agree that most of the powers attributed to Peter are assigned to the Church as a whole. But there are distinctions seemingly reserved for Peter. Peter alone is given the "keys to the kingdom of heaven" (16:19, a point by the way not directly addressed by Kingsbury's study) and called the "rock" on which the Church is built (16:18). And even though the disciples have confessed Jesus as Son of God in 14:33, Peter's confession is singled out and he is individually blessed as having received a revelation from the Father (16:17). It is difficult to see how such emphasis portrays Peter merely as "representative." Also, Brown and his colleagues emphasize that the burgeoning image of Peter in Matthew is not limited to his salvation-historical role in the period of Jesus' earthly existence but, as in the case of the temple tax (17:24–27) has to do with the resolution of problems for the *post-Easter* Church. Note, too, that in the story of the tax, a shekel is provided for Jesus and Peter (not for the community as a whole; see 17:27), another hint at Peter's singular importance.

Perhaps the most important contribution made by Brown and his colleagues is that they discuss Peter's role not only within the context of Matthew's Gospel (the focus of Kingsbury's study) but within the New Testament as a whole. Here they detect a Petrine "trajectory" which attributes increasing prominence to Peter's image as pastor, missionary, martyr, confessor of the faith, receiver of special revelation, and guardian of the faith, and also as a weak and sinful man.[13] Elements of this multiple image are found not only in Matthew's special tradition about Peter but in texts as diverse as John 21, Luke 5:1–11 and 22:31–32, many places in Acts, and in the two letters written in Peter's name. A parallel sort of trajectory develops around Paul, as can be seen in his image as martyr, pastor, and guardian of the faith in the pastoral epistles. But the Petrine trajectory became the dominant one, and in 2 Peter 3:15–16 we have an instance in which "Peter" is presented as the authentic interpreter of Pauline tradition. The full development of the Petrine trajectory takes us beyond the New Testament into early patristic writings.

In his essay, Brown suggests that it is not so much an individual piece of the Petrine tradition such as in Matthew's Gospel which bears crucial ecumenical implications as it is the development of the Petrine trajectory in which Matthew's text plays an important part. The trajectory itself may give us a better idea of the emerging ecclesial consciousness of early Christianity, and thus become a significant factor in on-going ecumenical dialogue. For our modest goal of understanding Matthew's portrayal of Peter, the notion of a developing Petrine tradition suggests that the apostle's role in the Gospel is not reducible to that of representative disciple or mere "salvation-history primacy" but may indeed stand as a symbol and model of developing functions of pastoral leadership in Matthew's church.

Conclusion

Despite points of debate still unresolved and frustration in finding a comprehensive theological framework for Matthew's ecclesiology, the aspects of the Gospel we have reviewed in this chapter truly confirm that the nature of communal Christian existence was of a pressing interest for this evangelist. Matthew's portrayal of the bond between the community and the risen Christ, his emphasis on ethical response, and his composite portrayal of Peter and the disciples are proof of a profound ecclesial sense.

Notes

Preface

1. Cf. W.G. Kümmel, *The New Testament: The History of the Investigation of Its Problems* (Nashville: Abingdon, 1972); D.J. Harrington, *Interpreting the New Testament: A Practical Guide* (New Testament Message 1; Wilmington, Del.: Michael Glazier, 1979).

2. Cf. W. Marxsen, *Mark the Evangelist* (Nashville: Abingdon, 1969), a translation of a German work that first appeared in 1956; H. Conzelmann, *The Theology of Saint Luke* (London: Faber & Faber, 1960), first appearing in German in 1953; G. Bornkamm, G. Barth, H.J. Held, *Tradition and Interpretation in Matthew* (Philadelphia: Westminster, 1963); Bornkamm's essay, "The Stilling of the Storm in Matthew," included in this collection, had already appeared in German in 1948. On the entire method of redaction criticism, cf. N. Perrin, *What Is Redaction Criticism?* (Guides to Biblical Scholarship; Philadelphia: Fortress, 1969).

3. Cf. W.G. Thompson, *Matthew's Advice to a Divided Community, Mt. 17, 22–18, 35* (Analecta Biblica 44; Rome: Biblical Institute, 1970), 12–13, and especially, "An Historical Perspective in the Gospel of Matthew," *Journal of Biblical Literature* 93 (1974) 244.

4. Cf. W.A. Beardslee, *Literary Criticism of the New Testament* (Guides to Biblical Scholarship; Philadelphia: Fortress, 1970).

5. See, for example, the work of S. TeSelle, *Speaking in Parables: A Study in Metaphor and Theology* (Philadelphia: Fortress, 1975).

6. A valuable overview of recent studies is D. Harrington's "Matthean Studies Since Joachim Rohde," *The Heythrop Journal* 16 (1975) 375–88.

Chapter 1

1. For an evaluation of Papias' statement, cf. W.G. Kümmel, *Introduction to the New Testament* (trans. by H.C. Kee; Nashville: Abingdon, rev. English ed., 1975) 120–21.

2. W.D. Davies, *The Setting of the Sermon on the Mount* (Cambridge: Cambridge University, 1964); a briefer and more popular version of Davies' work is *The Sermon on the Mount* (Cambridge: Cambridge University, 1966).

3. On the role of the Pharisees, cf. J. Neusner, *From Politics to Piety: The Emergence of Pharisaic Judaism* (Englewood Cliffs: Prentice-Hall, 1973) and by the same author, *First Century Judaism in Crisis* (Nashville: Abingdon, 1975). An account of the revolt and its aftermath through the writings of the first century historian Josephus is found in the work of D.M. Rhoads, *Israel in Revolution 6–74 C.E.* (Philadelphia: Fortress, 1976).

4. Quoted by Davies, *The Setting*, p. 275.

5. R. Hummel, *Die Auseinandersetzung zwischen Kirche und Judentum im Matthäusevangelium* ("The Division between Church and Judaism in the Gospel of Matthew"; München: Kaiser Verlag, 1963).

6. Cf. the similar viewpoint of M. Barth below.

7. D.R.A. Hare, *The Theme of Jewish Persecution of Christians in the Gospel According to St. Matthew* (Society for New Testament Studies Monograph Series 6; Cambridge: Cambridge University, 1967).

8. G. Strecker, *Der Weg der Gerechtigkeit: Untersuchung zur Theologie des Matthäus* (Göttingen: Vandenhoeck & Ruprecht, 2nd rev. ed., 1966).

9. R. Hummel, *Die Auseinandersetzung*.

10. D. Hare, *The Theme of Jewish Persecution*.

11. Poul Nepper-Christensen, *Das Matthäusevangelium. Ein judenchristliches Evangelium?* ("The Gospel of Matthew. A Jewish Christian Gospel?" Aarhus: Universitetsforlaget, 1958).

12. J.P. Meier, *The Vision of Matthew: Christ, Church and Morality in the First Gospel* (Theological Inquiries: New York: Paulist, 1979).

13. J.D. Kingsbury, *Matthew* (Proclamation Commentaries: Philadelphia: Fortress, 1977).

14. On the sources for Matthew's Gospel cf. below, Chapter II.

15. Cf. above.

16. Cf. the evaluation of these various suggestions in W.G. Kümmel, *Introduction to the New Testament*, pp. 119–20.

17. B.T. Viviano, "Where Was the Gospel According to Matthew Written?" *Catholic Biblical Quarterly* 41 (1979) 533–46.

18. On a possible "school" context for Matthew, cf. the discussion of K. Stendahl's thesis below.

19. Cf. below.

20. Cf. D. Senior, "The Ministry of Continuity: Matthew's Gospel and the Interpretation of History," *The Bible Today* 82 (1976) 670–76.

Chapter 2

1. For a discussion of the source question in the gospels, cf. D. Harrington, *Interpreting the New Testament: A Practical Guide* (New Testament Message 1; Wilmington: Michael Glazier, 1979).

2. Cf. the discussion in W.G. Kümmel, *Introduction to the New Testament,* pp. 63–76; J.D. Kingsbury, *Jesus Christ in Matthew, Mark, and Luke* (Proclamation Commentaries; Fortress: Philadelphia, 1981), pp. 1–27; R.A. Edwards, *A Theology of Q: Eschatology, Prophecy, and Wisdom* (Fortress: Philadelphia, 1975).

3. G. Bornkamm, "The Authority to 'Bind' and 'Loose' in the Church in Matthew's Gospel: The Problem of Sources in Matthew's Gospel," in *Jesus and Man's Hope* (Pittsburgh: Pittsburgh Theological Seminary, 1970), Volume I, pp. 37–50.

4. D. Senior, *The Passion Narrative According to Matthew: A Redactional Study* (Bibliotheca Ephemeridum Theologicarum Lovaniensium 39; Louvain: Louvain University, 1975).

5. B.C. Butler, *The Originality of St. Matthew: A Critique of the Two-Document Hypothesis* (Cambridge: Cambridge University, 1951).

6. William R. Farmer, *The Synoptic Problem: A Critical Analysis* (Dillsboro: Western North Carolina Press, 1976, a reprint of the 1964 edition, New York: Macmillan).

7. M.D. Goulder, *Midrash and Lection in Matthew* (London: SPCK, 1974).

8. W.F. Albright and C.S. Mann, *Matthew* (The Anchor Bible 26; Garden City: Doubleday, 1971).

9. Cf. a thorough discussion of the issue in F. Neirynck, *Minor Agreements of Matthew and Luke Against Mark, with a Consultative List* (Bibliotheca Ephemeridum Theologicarum Lovaniensium 37; Louvain: Louvain University, 1974).

10. W.G. Thompson, *Matthew's Advice to a Divided Community. Mt. 17,22–18,35* (Analecta Biblica 44; Rome: Biblical Institute, 1970).

11. B.W. Bacon, *Studies in Matthew* (London: Constable, 1930), and by the same author, "The 'Five Books' of Matthew against the Jews," *The Expositor* 15 (1918) 55–66.

12. Cf. the thorough discussion of this issue in W.D. Davies, *The Setting,* pp. 14–108.

13. H. Frankemölle, *Jahwebund und Kirche Christi* (Neutestamentliche Abhandlungen 10; Münster: Aschendorff, 1974).

14. P.F. Ellis, *Matthew: His Mind and His Message* (Collegeville: The Liturgical Press, 1974).

15. For a fuller presentation in schematic form of the chiastic patterns Ellis perceives in Matthew, cf. *ibid.,* p. 12.

16. J.D. Kingsbury, *Matthew: Structure, Christology, Kingdom* (Philadelphia: Fortress, 1975).

17. Donald Senior, *Invitation to Matthew* (Image Books; Garden City: Doubleday, 1977).

Chapter 3

1. On Matthew's use of the Old Testament, cf. below, Chapter IV.

2. Cf. the discussion of Matthew's milieu in Chapter I.

3. Rolf Walker, *Die Heilsgeschichte im ersten Evangelium* (Göttingen: Vandenhoeck & Ruprecht, 1967).

4. G. Strecker, "Das Geschichtsverständnis des Matthäus," *Evangelische Theologie* 26 (1966) 57–74; an English translation appeared in the *Journal of the American Academy of Religion* 35 (1967) 219–30.

5. Cf. the role of these same verses in the structure of Matthew, above, Chapter II.

6. J. Meier, "Salvation-History in Matthew: In Search of a Starting Point," *Catholic Biblical Quarterly* 37 (1975) 203–15; *Law and History in Matthew's Gospel: A Redactional Study of Mt. 5:17–48* (Analecta Biblica 71; Rome: Biblical Institute, 1976); *The Vision of Matthew* (1979).

7. J. Meier, *The Vision of Matthew,* p. 34.

8. For a discussion of this passage and its background in the Old Testament and Judaism, cf. D. Senior, "The Death of Jesus and the Resurrection of the Holy Ones (Mt 27:51–53)," *Catholic Biblical Quarterly* 38 (1976), 312–29.

9. J. Meier, *The Vision of Matthew,* p. 37.

10. On Matthew's attitude to the Jewish law, cf. below, Chapter IV.

11. J.D. Kingsbury, *Matthew: Structure, Christology, Kingdom,* pp. 1–39.

Chapter 4

1. On the best characterization of these special Old Testament quotations in Matthew, cf. W.G. Kümmel, *Introduction to the New Testament,* p. 110, n. 23. He argues that the term "fulfillment quotations" coined by Rothfuchs is preferable since it points to the function of the quotations. The term "formula quotations" has been used by scholars since the turn of the century. Some interpreters exclude 2:6 from the list because it does not have the term "fulfill" in the introductory formula, and 26:56 because it speaks of

the "Scriptures of the prophets" being fulfilled but does not cite any specific text. This verse from Matthew's passion narrative is similar to Mark 14:49 ("but let the Scriptures be fulfilled"); its application of the Old Testament to the events of the passion may have been an important starting point for Matthew's use of Old Testament fulfillment texts in application to other events of Jesus' life. On this cf. D. Senior, *The Passion Narrative,* 151–55.

2. K. Stendahl, *The School of St. Matthew and Its Use of the Old Testament* (Philadelphia: Fortress, first American ed. 1968).

3. Stendahl detects strict rules or guidelines that the Qumran community used in this type of scriptural interpretation; cf. *The School of St. Matthew,* pp. 191–92.

4. R.H. Gundry, *The Use of the Old Testament in St. Matthew's Gospel with Special Reference to the Messianic Hope* (Supplements to Novum Testamentum 18; Leiden: E.J. Brill, 1967).

5. Gundry elaborates on his reasons for the early dating of Matthew in his recent commentary, *Matthew: A Commentary on His Literary and Theological Art* (Grand Rapids: William B. Eerdmans, 1982), pp. 599–622.

6. W. Rothfuchs, *Die Erfüllungszitate des Matthäus-Evangeliums: Eine biblisch-theologische Untersuchung* (Beiträge zur Wissenschaft vom Alten und Neuen Testament 8; Stuttgart: W. Kohlhammer, 1969).

7. Cf. the discussion of Strecker's viewpoint, above, Chapter III.

8. Cf. J.D. Kingsbury, *The Parables of Jesus in Matthew 13: A Study in Redaction Criticism* (Richmond: John Knox, 1969), pp. 12–15; for a different approach to the entire parable discourse, cf. J. Dupont, "Le point de vue de Matthieu dans le chapitre des paraboles," in *L'Évangile selon Matthieu: Rédaction et Théologie* (ed. M. Didier; Bibliotheca Ephemeridum Theologicarum Lovaniensium 29; Gembloux: Duculot, 1972), pp. 221–60.

9. This is similar to the view of G.D. Kilpatrick, *The Origins of the Gospel According to St. Matthew* (Oxford: Clarendon, 1946).

10. F. Van Segbroeck, "Les citations d'accomplissement dans l'Évangile selon Matthieu d'après trois ouvrages récents," in *L'Évangile selon Matthieu* (ed. M. Didier), pp. 107–30.

11. A recent proponent of earlier dating for the Gospels and most of the New Testament books is J.A.T. Robinson in his work, *Redating the New Testament* (Philadelphia: Westminster, 1976). He claims that there is no evidence in the Gospels that the evangelists were aware of the destruction of Jerusalem, therefore all of them were written prior to A.D. 70.

12. For a thorough study of Matthew's use of Markan source material, cf. F. Neirynck, "La rédaction matthéenne et la structure du premier évangile," *Ephemerides Theologicae Lovanienses* 43 (1967) 41–73.

Chapter 5

1. This is true, for example, of the studies of R. Hammerton-Kelly (cf. below) and J. Meier, *The Vision of Matthew.* On the whole issue of the Jewish law and Christianity, cf. the thoughtful essay of W.D. Davies, "The Significance of the Law in Christianity," in *Christians and Jews* (eds. H. Küng and W. Kasper; *Concilium;* New York: Seabury, 1974), 24–32.

2. Most scholars agree that in these instances, the Matthean Jesus has radicalized the law to the point of contravening it; on this cf. J. Meier, *Law and History in Matthew's Gospel,* pp. 140–61.

3. G. Barth, "Matthew's Understanding of the Law," in *Tradition and Interpretation in Matthew* (Philadelphia: Westminster, 1963), 58–164.

4. This position is similar to that of R. Hummel, discussed above.

5. Cf. E. Schweizer, "Observance of the Law and Charismatic Activity in Matthew," *New Testament Studies* 16 (1970) 213–30.

6. R.G. Hammerton-Kelly, "Attitudes to the Law in Matthew's Gospel: a Discussion of Matthew 5:18," *Biblical Research* 17 (1972) 19–32.

7. See, for example, the works of A. Sand and J. Meier, discussed below.

8. R. Banks, "Matthew's Understanding of the Law: Authenticity and Interpretation in Matthew 5:17–20," *Journal of Biblical Literature* 93 (1974) 243–262; see also by the same author, *Jesus and the Law in the Synoptic Tradition* (Society for New Testament Studies Monograph Series 28; Cambridge: Cambridge University, 1975). In his book, Banks concentrates on the question of Jesus' own attitude to the law rather than the theology of Matthew.

9. R. Banks, "Matthew's Understanding of the Law," pp. 229–32.

10. A. Sand, *Das Gesetz und die Propheten: Untersuchungen zur Theologie des Evangeliums nach Matthäus* (Biblische Untersuchungen 11; Regensburg: Friedrich Pustet, 1974).

11. On the background and use of this key term in Matthew, cf. B. Przybylski, *Righteousness in Matthew and His World of Thought* (Society for New Testament Studies Monograph Series 41; Cambridge: Cambridge University, 1980).

12. For full references to these works, cf. above.

13. J. Meier, *The Vision of Matthew,* p. 262.

Chapter 6

1. On the role of titles for Jesus in New Testament Christology, cf. R.H. Fuller, *The Foundations of New Testament Christology* (New York:

Charles Scribner's Sons, 1965) and F. Hahn, *The Titles of Jesus in Christology* (London: Lutterworth, 1969).

2. J.D. Kingsbury, *Matthew: Structure, Christology, Kingdom* (Philadelphia: Fortress, 1975), esp. 40–127, and his more recent work, *Jesus Christ in Matthew, Mark, and Luke*, pp. 64–73.

3. On Davidic motifs in Matthew, particularly in the infancy narrative, cf. B.M. Nolan, *The Royal Son of God: The Christology of Matthew 1–2 in the Setting of the Gospel* (Orbis Biblicus et Orientalis 23; Göttingen: Vandenhoeck & Ruprecht, 1979).

4. See, for example, G. Strecker, *Der Weg der Gerechtigkeit*, pp. 123–26, and W. Trilling, *Das Wahre Israel: Studien zur Theologie des Matthäus-Evangeliums* (München: Kösel, 3rd ed., 1964), pp. 21–51.

5. D. Hill, "Son and Servant: An Essay on Matthean Christology," *Journal for the Study of the New Testament* 6 (1980) 2–16.

6. On the role of Isaiah 42:1–4 in this passage, see the study of L. Cope, *Matthew: A Scribe Trained for the Kingdom of Heaven* (The Catholic Biblical Quarterly Monograph Series 5; Washington: Catholic Biblical Association of America, 1976), pp. 32–51.

7. Cf. B. Gerhardsson, *The Mighty Acts of Jesus According to Matthew* (Lund: CWK Gleerup, 1979), esp. 88–91.

8. John Meier, *The Vision of Matthew*, pp. 210–19.

9. M.J. Suggs, *Wisdom, Christology, and Law in Matthew's Gospel* (Cambridge: Harvard University, 1970).

10. On the Wisdom tradition in Israel, see the excellent introduction by G. von Rad, *Wisdom in Israel* (New York: Abingdon, 1973).

11. On this point, cf. J. Dunn, *Christology in the Making: A New Testament Inquiry into the Origins of the Doctrine of the Incarnation* (Philadelphia: Westminster, 1980), esp., pp. 163–212.

12. M.D. Johnson, "Reflections on a Wisdom Approach to Matthew's Christology," *Catholic Biblical Quarterly* 36 (1974) 44–64.

13. F.W. Burnett, *The Testament of Jesus-Sophia: A Redaction-Critical Study of the Eschatological Discourse in Matthew* (Washington: University Press of America, 1981).

14. Cf. R. Brown, *The Gospel According to John I–XII* (The Anchor Bible 29; Garden City: Doubleday, 1966), pp. cxxii–cxxv; and J. Dunn, *Christology in the Making, ibid.*

15. H.J. Held, "Matthew as Interpreter of the Miracle Stories," in *Tradition and Interpretation in Matthew*, pp. 165–299.

16. See, for example, W.G. Thompson, "Reflections on the Composition of Mt. 8:1–9:34," *Catholic Biblical Quarterly* 33 (1971) 365–388, and

J.P. Heil, "Significant Aspects of the Healing Miracles in Matthew," *Catholic Biblical Quarterly* 41 (1979) 274–87.

17. J.D. Kingsbury, "Observations on the 'Miracle Chapters' of Matthew 8–9," *Catholic Biblical Quarterly* 40 (1978) 559–73.

18. C. Burger, "Jesu Taten nach Matthäus 8 und 9," *Zeitschrift für Theologie und Kirche* 70 (1973) 272–73.

19. B. Gerhardsson, *The Mighty Acts of Jesus According to Matthew.*

Chapter 7

1. H. Frankemölle, *Jahwebund und Kirche Christi.*

2. For a broader discussion of the form and possible Old Testament background of Matthew 28:16–20, cf. B.J. Hubbard, *The Matthean Redaction of a Primitive Apostolic Commissioning: An Exegesis of Matthew 28:16–20* (SBL Dissertation Series 19; Missoula: Society of Biblical Literature, 1974).

3. Cf. J.D. Kingsbury's critique of Frankemölle on this point in *Matthew: Structure, Christology, Kingdom,* pp. 37–39.

4. On the role of the disciples in Matthew, cf. G. Barth, *Tradition and Interpretation in Matthew,* pp. 105–24; U. Luz, "Die Jünger im Matthäusevangelium," *Zeitschrift für Neuentestamentliche Wissenschaft* 62 (1971) 141–71; M. Sheridan, "Disciples and Discipleship in Matthew and Luke," *Biblical Theology Bulletin* 3 (1973) 235–55.

5. J. Zumstein, *La Condition du Croyant dans L'Évangile selon Matthieu* (Orbis Biblicus et Orientalis 16; Göttingen: Vandenhoeck & Ruprecht, 1977).

6. On this, see P. Minear, "The Disciples and Crowds in the Gospel of Matthew," *Anglican Theological Review* Supplementary Series 3 (1974) 28–43.

7. See S. Van Tilborg, *The Jewish Leaders in Matthew* (Leiden: E.J. Brill, 1972).

8. On the community discourse of Matthew 18 as an important source for his ecclesiology, cf. W.G. Thompson, *Matthew's Advice to a Divided Community,* and W. Pesch, *Matthäus der Seelsorger: Das neue Verständnis der Evangelien dargestellet am Beispiel von Matthäus 18* (Stuttgarter Bibel-Studien 2; Stuttgart: Katholisches Bibelwerk, 1966).

9. J.D. Kingsbury, "The Figure of Peter in Matthew's Gospel as a Theological Problem," *Journal of Biblical Literature* 98 (1979) 67–83.

10. *Ibid.,* pp. 72–74.

11. R. Brown, K. Donfried, J. Reumann (eds.), *Peter in the New Testa-*

ment: A Collaborative Assessment by Protestant and Roman Catholic Scholars (Minneapolis: Augsburg/New York: Paulist, 1973).

12. R. Brown, *Biblical Reflections on Crises Facing the Church* (New York: Paulist, 1975), 63–83.

13. *Peter in the New Testament,* pp. 162–68.